D1523090

Healthy Teens, Healthy Schools

Healthy Teens, Healthy Schools

*How Media Literacy Education Can
Renew Education in the United States*

Vanessa Domine

ROWMAN & LITTLEFIELD
Lanham • Boulder • New York • London

Published by Rowman & Littlefield
A wholly owned subsidiary of The Rowman & Littlefield Publishing Group, Inc.
4501 Forbes Boulevard, Suite 200, Lanham, Maryland 20706
www.rowman.com

Unit A, Whitacre Mews, 26-34 Stannary Street, London SE11 4AB

British Library Cataloguing in Publication Information Available

Library of Congress Cataloging-in-Publication Data

Domine, Vanessa Elaine.
Healthy teens, healthy schools : how media literacy education can renew education in the United States / Vanessa Domine.
pages cm.
Includes bibliographical references and index.
ISBN 978-1-4758-1356-2 (cloth : alk. paper) — ISBN 978-1-4758-1358-6 (pbk. : alk. paper) — ISBN 978-1-4758-1359-3 (electronic)
1. Health education—United States. 2. Schools—Health promotion services—United States. 3. Students—Health and hygiene—United States. 4. Media literacy—Study and teaching—United States. I. Title.
LB1588.U6D66 2015
371.7'10973—dc23

                                    2015009667

∞ ™ The paper used in this publication meets the minimum requirements of American National Standard for Information Sciences Permanence of Paper for Printed Library Materials, ANSI/NISO Z39.48-1992.

Printed in the United States of America

Contents

Acknowledgments

I extend my gratitude and admiration to all the educators and public health professionals who are doing the important work of health literacy promotion worldwide. Thank you to my inspiring colleagues at the National Association for Media Literacy Education who each in their own way planted the seeds of an idea for this book—especially Tina Peterson, Lynda Bergsma, and Faith Rogow. I also extend my appreciation to my current academic home of Montclair State University for awarding me a semester-long sabbatical to start this book. And thanks to myself for the extra year of hard work and sacrifice to actually finish writing it.

A knuckle bump to David Keiser in the Department of Secondary and Special Education at Montclair State University for being a critical friend in reviewing drafts of chapters and for being an eternally optimistic and supportive colleague. I also extend my thanks to my cherubic graduate assistants who have assisted me with the research for this book, including Mary Fuchs, Kevin Christman, Michelle Thomas, and Michele Messina. Their impressive work ethic and keen eyes for detail sustained me throughout the research and writing process.

I wrote this book in memory of my father, whose heart ultimately failed him, but mostly to honor my mother, whose heart has never failed me. I dedicate this book to my four delicious children in the hope that each of them will intentionally and diligently seek (and obtain) health and happiness across their lifetime.

Introduction

One February morning in Invercargill, New Zealand, Natasha Harris helped her children get ready for school. Harris, a thirty-year-old mother of eight, had not been feeling well for months. She was lethargic and had been chronically vomiting. On this particular morning in 2010, her family discovered her slumped in the bathroom, gasping for air. Harris had suffered a cardiac arrhythmia and ultimately could not be revived. Although her family initially thought her death was caused by ill health and the normal stress associated with raising eight children, they learned there was much more to the story.

A pathology report indicated Harris had extremely low blood potassium levels consistent with her symptoms of tiredness and lack of strength leading up to her death. She also had an enlarged liver with fatty deposits, indicating chronic and excessive sugar intake. Further investigation revealed that Harris was addicted to the popular soda beverage Coca-Cola, or Coke, drinking two gallons of it every day over the course of eight years. This amount equated to more than two pounds (or eleven times the recommended daily amount) of sugar and 970 milligrams (or twice the recommended safe amount) of caffeine.

A postmortem investigation revealed that Coke was the first thing Harris drank in the morning and the last thing she consumed before going to sleep. Harris also suffered from a nicotine addiction. She reportedly smoked around thirty cigarettes a day and ate very little food, suggesting that her death was a result of a confluence of addiction and ailments across time. Yet, when the coroner released his report three years after Harris's death, he identified Coke as the major culprit:

> More likely than not the drinking of large quantities of Coke was a substantial factor that contributed to the development of the metabolic imbalances which gave rise to the arrhythmia. . . . [W]ere it not for the consumption of very large quantities of Coke . . . it is unlikely that she would have died when she died and how she died.[1]

The coroner clarified that while Coca-Cola "cannot be held responsible for the health of consumers who drink unhealthy quantities of the product," he suggested that the company consider placing warning labels on their products:

> The hazards to the health of the consumers of excessive quantities of sugar and caffeine contained in carbonated drinks could be more clear-

1

ly emphasised [sic]. . . . Consideration should be given . . . to either
lowering the caffeine percentage limit or creating a more specific warning such as those printed on [energy drinks] produced and marketed
by Coca-Cola.[2]

The coroner's report generated controversy worldwide: News outlets
circulated the headlines: "Coke kills Mum," "Death by Coke," and "Coke
overdose?" In response to the publicity, Coca-Cola released an official
statement:

> [We] are disappointed that the coroner has chosen to focus on the
> combination of Ms. Harris' excessive consumption of Coca-Cola, to-
> gether with other health and lifestyle factors, as the probable cause of
> her death. . . . In this case, a warning label would not have made much
> difference. The truth is there would not be a warning label on the
> planet that would have dealt with this extreme consumption. You can't
> label for extremes.[3]

While the coroner identified Coke as the major variable in Harris's death,
he also underscored the accountability of Harris and her family:

> The fact [Harris] had her teeth extracted several years before her death
> because of what her family believed was Coke-induced tooth decay,
> and the fact that one or more of her children were born without enamel
> on their teeth, should have been treated by her, and by her family, as a
> warning.[4]

Harris's mother also acknowledged the ultimate accountability of her
daughter, stating: "It was [Natasha's] choice to drink Coke. She didn't
like water or tea or coffee, and she didn't eat much either, and that had a
lot to do with it."[5] Given Harris's health profile, it is questionable the
extent to which a warning label on a Coke bottle would have made much
of a difference.

It is curious that neither Harris nor her family members heeded the
visible warning signs leading up to her death. Harris's partner, Chris
Hodgkinson, lamented in an interview: "I never considered [Coke]
would do any harm to a person. It's just a soft drink, just like drinking
water. . . . I didn't think a drink's going to kill you."[6] Only in hindsight
did he acknowledge the warning signs:

> We used to joke about that Coke would do harm to her, I suppose, but I
> didn't realize that it actually would. . . . [T]hat's just what she drunk.
> She just had to have it. . . . Definitely people need to get aware of what
> it can do, especially towards what it could be doing to small kids.[7]

Although Harris's case is extreme, the affinity to Coca-Cola is not
exceptional. Cultural studies scholars assert that Coca-Cola is much more
than a soft drink; it is a microcosm of American history. On any given
day, 1.8 billion servings of a Coca-Cola beverage are consumed around
the world, and 94 percent of the world's population recognizes the Coca-

Cola logo. Not only does Coca-Cola have more Facebook fans (forty-two million) than any other brand, but the annual US$47.5 billion revenue generated by Coca-Cola is more than the gross domestic product of Haiti, Malawi, Jamaica, and Afghanistan combined.

While the path of least resistance may be to blame for Natasha Harris's irresponsible and unhealthy choices, her death calls attention to a disturbing disconnection between the conditions, contexts, and consumer habits that shape the health behaviors of individuals and the larger social, political, and economic environments in which they enact those behaviors.

In December 2011, fourteen-year-old Anais Fournier drank a twenty-four-ounce Monster energy drink while hanging out with her friends at a shopping mall in Maryland. The next day, she drank a second one and subsequently went into cardiac arrest and died six days later. The medical examiner listed the official cause of death as cardiac arrhythmia due to caffeine toxicity. At first this seemed logical: Fournier had consumed 480 milligrams of caffeine (or five times the daily limit recommended by the American Academy of Pediatrics), essentially equivalent to the amount of caffeine in fourteen cans of Coke. But there was more to the story.

Anais had a family history of heart problems that included an enlarged heart, a connective tissue disease, and mitral valve prolapse. When her family filed a lawsuit against Monster in October 2012, experts refuted the allegation that Anais died from caffeine toxicity and instead suggested that she suffered from inflammation of the heart that in turn increased her risk of sudden death independent of the caffeine she consumed. The Fournier family's attorney counterargued that Anais's death was hastened by the combination of caffeine and other caffeine-containing ingredients, such as guarana. Ultimately, a California judge ordered the case resolved through mediation, attributing merit to both sides of the argument.

While we must acknowledge the complexities of Anais's heart problems, at the same time we must not ignore the larger institutional contradiction that exists: Corporations aggressively market energy drinks to teenagers despite the warning labels that clearly state children should not consume them. In fact, energy drinks are highly popular among adolescent youth. Between 2001 and 2006 the sale of energy drinks rose by more than 400 percent, reaching sales of US$3.23 billion. Although soda and sugary drink consumption decreased among young children between 2009 and 2012, the consumption of sports and energy drinks by adolescents increased by 7 percent. Yet, the U.S. Food and Drug Administration (FDA) defines energy drinks as dietary supplements rather than a food item and therefore does not subject them to regulation. This bureaucratic schism poses a significant risk to our adolescent youth population.

If we dismiss the deaths of Natasha Harris and Anais Fournier as simply isolated tragedies of imperfect individuals making poor choices, we fail to examine the larger ecosystem of historical, social, political, and global economic forces that regulate the health of all individuals. Beyond Coca-Cola and Monster drinks exists a multiplicity of images, slogans, products, and virtual experiences within our modern world that collectively portray health and happiness while frequently producing the opposite results. On one hand, the belief that an individual has the ultimate choice and accountability aligns poignantly with the American Dream of freedom, economic prosperity, and social mobility. At the same time, by placing singular responsibility for health on the individual, we fail to hold accountable those institutional structures that disable individual agency and impede our ability to enact healthy behaviors.

THE PURSUIT OF HEALTH LITERACY

Since the 1940s the World Health Organization (WHO) and its member states have promoted good health as one of the fundamental rights of every human being. Health is much more than the mere absence of illness or disease; it is a state of complete physical, mental, and social well-being. Currently the Institute of Medicine, the American Medical Association, and the WHO define *health literacy* as the ability to obtain, process, and understand health information and services necessary to make appropriate health decisions.[8] Common examples of health literacy include the ability to treat common illnesses at home; to schedule a doctor's appointment; to understand an informed consent document; to read a prescription label; to maintain oral health; and to prevent obesity. It requires the ability to speak, write, listen, compute, and achieve conceptual understanding.

Successful navigation of the current healthcare system requires an increasingly complex set of skills that include understanding graphs or visual information, operating a computer, evaluating the credibility and truthfulness of health information, analyzing the risks and benefits of a particular treatment, and interpreting test results. From this standpoint, health literacy is inextricably connected to information literacy.

Based on this common, medical-oriented definition of health literacy, nearly half the adult American population (roughly ninety million) is health illiterate. More than one-third of U.S. adults have difficulty understanding vital warnings on the label of an over-the-counter medicine, and only 12 percent of adults are proficient enough to understand and use health information effectively.[9] To increase health literacy, the U.S. government in 2010 passed the Plain Writing Act that required health communications material to be simplified to a tenth-grade English reading level. Still, the national data show that thirty million Americans can only read English at a fifth-grade level.[10] From this standpoint, health literacy is inextricably connected to print literacy.

Clinicians say that print literacy can be a stronger predictor of an individual's health status than income, employment status, education level, race, or even ethnicity.[11] Others argue that print literacy isn't necessarily prerequisite to health literacy if individuals can speak, listen, and stand up for themselves.[12] We know that those who possess below-average health literacy are less likely to rely on written materials (including those on the Internet) and more likely to rely on radio or television, healthcare professionals, family, friends, or coworkers for health information.[13] This generates a need for health literacy across multiple forms of communication media.

According to the U.S. federal government, a health-literate America exists when "people are able to accurately assess the credibility of health information presented by health advocates, commercial and new media sources."[14] This is a challenge, given that individuals are continuously steeped in information that is brief, highly constructed, and often contradictory. Health information is produced and distributed by many different and often competing sources, including government, food and drug industries, and corporate marketers. Even individuals who are highly print literate have difficulty accessing, analyzing, and evaluating health information.

Current tools used by healthcare providers to measure adolescent health literacy measure only written comprehension and not critical thinking or decision-making abilities.[15] Adolescent youth may understand nutrition or prescription labels and be active, critical minded, and independent. Yet there is also a risk for such analytical ability to morph into dependence and even overreliance on scientific expertise. Up to 75 percent of teens that access the Internet use it to look for health-related information and do so either before *or instead of* consulting with a physician.[16]

Health literacy requires extracting information, comprehending its credibility and relevance, analyzing it effectively, and using it for one's own benefit and for the benefit of society. The FDA acknowledges that everyone deserves "to be taught in the fundamentals of how evidence is gathered in medicine as a matter of public education and public health, and how to evaluate its quality."[17] The FDA also indicates that individuals deserve to know "when we are being marketed to and who stands to profit from the treatments we take."[18] Consumers must therefore apply equally vigorous and critical analysis and evaluation of FDA practices as applied to the mass media marketing of Monster energy drinks and other Coca-Cola products. Indeed, health literacy in the twenty-first century requires critical decision making across the contexts and complexities of everyday life.

The significant increase in mass mediated messages about health over the past two decades has generated an increased sense of urgency for *media* literacy—not just among healthcare patients but also among the general population. Ultimately, conceptualizing health literacy as merely an extension of print literacy does not fully address the socioeconomic and political contexts that shape health. These and other concerns about the link between limited print literacy and low health literacy compel educators and policymakers to find ways to draw on newer forms of literacy, including digital literacies that involve blogging, texting, remixing, and other transmedia platforms.

A Media Literate Approach to Health

According to the National Association for Media Literacy Education (NAMLE), media literacy consists of "the habits of inquiry and skills of expression that individuals need to be critical thinkers, effective communicators and active citizens in today's world."[19] Just as health is not solely determined by how much food a person consumes, media literacy is not solely determined by how many media messages a person can critically evaluate. While the ability to critically analyze media texts (i.e., to identify the motives of junk food advertisers, deconstruct a pharmaceutical advertisement, etc.) is imperative, media literacy requires the active *creating and sharing* of information.[20] A core principle of media literacy is that individuals of all ages can creatively produce media messages, in addition to critically evaluating them. By being media producers and distributors, young people in particular can offer their interpretation of reality as agents of positive social change for healthy behavior.

The first step on the road to becoming both media and health literate is to understand that companies like Coca-Cola, Inc. are more invested in product sales than in the health of consumers.[21] Clay Johnson writes in *The Information Diet* that information obesity can lead to actual obesity.[22] Consumers therefore need to make wise information choices in addition to wise food choices. But to say that information literacy is an anti-information movement, or that media literacy is an anti-media movement, is just as misguided as saying that the crusade to end obesity is an anti-food movement. Akin to understanding the origins of food and possessing the skills to cook a healthy meal, media literacy requires a balanced approach to media through both critical consumption and creative production of messages about health—and then enactment of behaviors that are aligned with that understanding.

A major challenge is that media literacy interventions have greater effects on *knowledge* about media and health than they have on *attitudes* and *behavior*.[23] Health literacy or even critical thinking about health does not necessarily lead to behavioral change, which is a core function of health promotion. Additionally, the conversation about health literacy has primarily been the work of medical health professionals focusing mainly on adult patients being able to decode written information and interpret information to comply with doctor's orders. In this sense, the predominant understanding of health literacy is based on a deficit model: solving a problem, treating an illness, and/or curing a disease.

Catalyzing health illiteracy in the United States therefore necessitates a paradigm shift away from the current definition of health as the discovery and facilitation of treatments and cures for disease to a definition that compels the active construction of health. A media literate approach to health requires contextualizing choices and behaviors according to external factors of influence while also taking responsibility for one's own health and the health of families and communities.

A Focus on Adolescence

Over the past century, we have come to understand the adolescent youth population as a group that is both physiologically and psychologically different from children and adults. During adolescence, the brain increases in connectivity, which in turn enhances memory growth and literacy development. There is an increased urgency and intensity of emotional reactions, and the body undergoes hormonal changes related to reproduction as well as stress. While the teen brain does not resemble that of an adult until the early twenties, the individual learning capacity is never greater than during adolescence.[24] Teens are in the prime of developing their critical faculties. The rapid cognitive, physiological, and social development of a teenager poses great challenges yet also provides an open window of opportunity for educators. Research indicates that adolescents are able to:

- Generate more than one complex mental representation
- Appreciate the uncertainty of knowledge
- Think abstractly
- Plan and evaluate alternative strategies for obtaining knowledge
- Reflect on their own thought processes
- Evaluate the credibility of knowledge sources[25]

Teens are also developing skills and habits that will carry over through adulthood. The formative years of adolescence necessitate that the teenager establish a sense of identity; secure independence from parents; finish formal schooling; formulate plans for a career or job; and learn how to establish relationships with peers.

The tumultuous period of adolescence may exacerbate existing or emergent problems including obesity, eating disorders, poor nutrition, emotional problems, violence, unintentional injury, substance use, sexual promiscuity, and/or relationship problems. The symptoms of many mental and behavioral health disorders also first emerge during adolescence.

While there are physiological components to adolescence, there are also heavy influences of social, political, and economic forces at play. Teenagers of both sexes are regarded as a highly profitable consumer market. This developmental window of adolescence is a huge window of opportunity for advertisers to capitalize on brand awareness and brand loyalty. Researchers situate twelve- to fourteen-year-olds as "highly vulnerable" to advertising for unhealthy products as they have their own money to spend, are susceptible to impulsive behavior, and are beginning to separate from their parents.[26]

What adults consider to be "good" and "bad" for teens is usually in conflict with what corporations sell and the values imbued by mass media content. Researchers acknowledge that social structures and norms often work against rational health-related decision making among adolescents and that a more fruitful approach is to change the contexts in which risky behavior occurs rather than changing the way adolescents think about risk, for example.[27] Adolescents are generally more impulsive and self-conscious than adults and therefore they may be especially attracted to risky branded products that, in their view, provide immediate gratification, thrills, and/or social status. The vulnerability of adolescence implies that federal policy should protect teens from advertising and promotions for high-risk, addictive products, within constitutional limits. On the other hand, how do educators equip teenagers to successfully navigate the social, moral, and political turbulence that lies ahead of them as adults?

The control of disease and increased nutrition over the past two centuries have influenced an earlier onset of puberty and thus lengthened the period of adolescence. There is much we can learn from teens about media and healthy literacy as they transition into adulthood during a pivotal time in history. While large bodies of literature exist on the topics of adult health and physical activity among children, there is, in comparison, a paucity of research on *adolescent* health.

As adults, our perspective of adolescent youth is both complex and contradictory. Thomas Hine, author of *The Rise and Fall of the American Teenager*, eloquently describes this tension:

> Our beliefs, about teenagers are deeply contradictory: They should be free to become themselves. They need many years of training and study. They know more about the future than adults do. They know hardly anything at all. They ought to know the value of a dollar. They should be protected from the world of work. They are frail, vulnerable creatures. They are children. They are sex fiends. They are the death of culture. They are the hope of us all.[28]

Cultivating healthy teens requires a shift in our attitudes and understanding of adolescent youth populations as vulnerable yet moral agents that are capable of critical thought and positive health behaviors. Reframing health literacy through media literacy in schools can make all the difference.

HEALTHY TEENS THROUGH HEALTHY SCHOOLS

Schooling remains one of the primary institutions of socialization for adolescent youth as they navigate their way to adulthood. Not yet legally adults, teenagers are still children with all the protections afforded under the law. Because schools are inextricably connected to the social, economic, and political systems, they are shaped by a variety of competing agendas. The history of public schooling in the United States is indeed one of dissent and frequent conflict between the rights of the family and the responsibility of public schools to educate youth, especially on matters related to health. In this way, public schools are frequently described as one of the last bastions of democracy.

In 1967 the School Health Education Study reported an "appalling" state of health education in U.S. schools. The study called for a comprehensive program to address the physical, social, mental, economic, and cultural factors of health. It also framed health as a shared responsibility of individuals, communities, and world nations. In schools, health education has played out in the forms of driver's education, alcohol and drug prevention, sex education, and business education, among others. However, these policy-driven initiatives are frequently decontextualized and disconnected from the core subject area curriculum. Public schools have emerged as compartmentalized places that privilege literacy (reading and writing) and computation (mathematics) skills at the expense of their practical value.

On one hand is the elevation of expectations for student academic achievement and economic success, while the other hand segregates and isolates the health and well-being of children. Although there are federal and state curriculum mandates in the area of physical education, physical activity and movement is given short shrift during the school day. Within the walls of the school building are also contradictory messages about the importance of health and physical education. Formal health curricula define and promote nutritional standards while school cafeterias, vending machines, and advertisements provide easy access to substandard fare.

The public purpose of education and schooling is to help young people see health not as an object to be acquired, but rather as a means of living and of seeing the world. As educators our collective task is to move beyond warning labels to empower young people with critical habits of mind that in turn govern healthy minds, bodies, and ultimately schools. While it is true that young people are faced with a constellation of challenges to their successful growth and transition into adulthood even before they enter a classroom, a warning label approach is insufficient in preparing adolescent youth for the complexities of modern society. It is through examining the media ecology of adolescent health that we can begin to understand those forces that promote and also deter the health of our most promising yet at-risk population.

ABOUT THIS BOOK

Healthy Teens, Healthy Schools is for educators, parents, health professionals, and community leaders who assume their important role to create and sustain a healthier and more just society, one student and one school at a time. The book expands the traditional medical-focused concept of health literacy to focus on adolescent experiences that include school, social media, and technologized experiences. I echo the prominent voices of health literacy scholars worldwide, including Joan Wharf Higgins, Deborah Begoray, Ray Marks, Donald Nutbeam, and Lawrence St. Leger in their call for health education in schools to be interdisciplinary and inextricably connected to media literacy.

My specific purpose here is to reframe health education as inextricably connected to the choices of imperfect individuals within inequitable social structures. The goal is for the reader to achieve a more complete understanding of health literacy through the pedagogical method of media literacy. Social justice is an essential lever to increase healthy practices across individuals and communities, particularly those that are socioeconomically oppressed.

The theoretical framework for this exploration is social constructivism, which situates all learners as creators of their own understanding. At the same time, those understandings are shaped by environmental, social, and institutional circumstances. The pedagogical assumption here is that formal education must engage or activate learners instead of merely "delivering" curriculum. I therefore follow a long standing educational model that rejects the traditional delivery model of schooling in favor of a more democratic and agency-oriented set of practices that ultimately scaffold positive health behaviors among adolescent youth.

To this end, chapter 1 paints a statistical picture of the current climate in the United States that is anything but conducive to health among our adolescent population. The lack of a clear understanding of the cause(s) and solution(s) to the global pandemic of obesity is microcosmic of our inability as a nation to connect the dots in ways that are meaningful to the individual. While a national snapshot is disturbing, it is only as valid as the undergirding statistics. In a sea of statistical change is the constancy of critical inquiry, which is the foundation of media literacy and healthy behaviors.

Chapter 2 offers a media history of adolescent health to illustrate the ways in which our technological landscape has evolved into one that simultaneously opposes and promotes health. The chapter weaves together the histories of media and technology development alongside the emergence of adolescent youth culture to form a cultural tapestry of protectionism that may appear on the surface as morally imperative but may ultimately stunt the development of health literacy.

Chapter 3 outlines the principles and practices of media literacy education, which is not just *what* young people learn about health through media and education but also *how* they learn about health. I provide an agency-oriented pedagogical approach to health literacy that relies on the active engagement of adolescent youth as individuals within a diverse social, political, and economic ecosystem.

Chapter 4 disentangles several key threads of research, legislation, and policy that have impacted adolescent health education. It examines local and federal policies (where they exist) to increase health literacy among the U.S. population, including Michelle Obama's national efforts to improve school lunch programs and increase physical activity among young people. While anti-tobacco, anti-alcohol, and anti-junk food campaigns have, for the most part, served the public well, the pedagogical approach has been limited to countercultural resistance that goes against status quo, rather than reshaping it.

Chapter 5 calls attention to the marginalization of health and physical education in schools as collateral damage from the decades-long emphasis on standardized testing. The chapter moves beyond the deficit model of health literacy to remind educators of the power and possibility of whole school and interdisciplinary approaches that involve multiple stakeholders. Conceptualizing media literacy as a pedagogical method is a bridge to an interdisciplinary understanding of health.

Chapter 6 highlights pockets of innovation involving collaborative efforts of communities, schools, families, and advocacy groups that have emerged in recent years in response to the call for increased health literacy within at-risk populations. The chapter also illustrates how these community programs and practices can serve as a bridge to authentic health and media literacy experiences both inside and outside the school classroom.

NOTES

1. "Coca-Cola Drinking 'Linked to New Zealander's Death,'" *BBC News Asia*, February 12, 2013, http://www.bbc.co.uk/news/world-asia-21423499.

2. "Too Much Coke Killed Mum," *Stuff.co.nz*, February 13, 2013, http://www.stuff.co.nz/nelson-mail/news/8295575/Too-much-Coke-killed-mum.

3. Evan Harding and Sam Boyer, "Woman's Coca-Cola Addiction Deadly," *Southland Times*, February 13, 2013, 1:03, http://www.stuff.co.nz/southland-times/news/8293658/Womans-Coca-Cola-addiction-deadly.

4. "Coca-Cola Drinking."

5. "Too Much Coke."

6. "Natasha Harris Died from Drinking Too Much Coke, New Zealand Coroner Says," *The Huffington Post*, February 12, 2013 [video]: 41, http://www.huffingtonpost.com/2013/02/12/natasha-harris-died-too-much-coke-new-zealand-coroner_n_2671931.html.

7. "Too Much Coke."

8. Kristine Sorensen, Stephan Van den Broucke, James Fullam, Gerardine Doyle, Jürgen Pelikan, Zofia Slonska, and Helmut Brand, "Health Literacy and Public Health: A Systematic Review and Integration of Definitions and Models," *BMC Public Health* 12, no. 80 (2012), http://www.biomedcentral.com/1471-2458/12/80.

9. Shieda White, *Assessing the Nation's Health Literacy: Key Concepts and Findings of the National Assessment of Adult Literacy (NAAL)*. American Medical Association, 2008, xiii, http://www.amafoundation.org/go/healthliteracy.

10. HealthWorks Collective, "The Facts about Health Literacy in the United States," December 27, 2012, http://healthworkscollective.com/73026/health-literacy-us.

11. Barry D. Weiss, *Health Literacy and Patient Safety: Help Patients Understand: Manual for Clinicians*, 2nd ed. American Medical Association Foundation, 2007.

12. Susie Sykes, Jane Wills, Gillian Rowlands, and Keith Popple, "Understanding Critical Health Literacy: A Concept Analysis," *BMC Public Health* 13, no. 150 (February 18, 2013), doi: 10.1186/1471-2458-13-150.

13. White, *Assessing the Nation's Health Literacy*, xiii.

14. Lynn Nielsen-Bohlman, Allison M. Panzer, David A. and Kindig, eds., *Health Literacy: A Prescription to End Confusion*. Washington, DC: National Academies Press, 2004.

15. National Institute for Health Care Management (NIHCM), "The Case for Investing in Youth Health Literacy: One Step on the Path to Achieving Health Equity for Adolescents." Washington, DC: NIHCM Foundation, October 2011, 6.

16. Michele Ybarra and Michael Suman, "Reasons, Assessments, and Actions Taken: Sex and Age Differences in the Uses of Internet Health Information," *Health Education Research* 23, no. 3 (2008): 512–21.

17. Baruch Fischhoff, Noel T. Brewer, and Julie S. Downs, eds., *Communicating Risks and Benefits: An Evidence-Based User's Guide*. Silver Spring, MD: U.S. Department of Health and Human Services Food and Drug Administration, August 2011.

18. Fischhoff, Brewer, and Downs, *Communicating Risks and Benefits*.

19. National Association for Media Literacy Education, "Core Principles of Media Literacy Education," 2007, http://namle.net/wp-content/uploads/2013/01/CorePrinciples.pdf.

20. Renee Hobbs, *Digital and Media Literacy: A Plan of Action*. Washington, DC: The Aspen Institute, 2010, http://www.knightcomm.org/digital-and-media-literacy-a-plan-of-action.

21. In August 2014, Coca-Cola announced that it would pay Monster US$2.15 billion for a 16.7 percent share in the company. Coca-Cola will also gain two seats on the Monster board of directors. See Maggie McGrath, "Coca-Cola Buys Stake in Monster Beverage for $2 Billion," *Forbes*, August 14, 2014, http://www.forbes.com/sites/maggiemcgrath/2014/08/14/coca-cola-buys-stake-in-monster-beverage-for-2-billion/.

22. Clay A. Johnson, "Information Obesity and Food Obesity," *The Information Diet: A Case for Conscious Consumption* (blog), July 28, 2010, http://www.informationdiet.com/blog/read/information-obesity-and-food-obesity.

23. Se-Hoon Jeong, Hyunyi Cho, and Yoori Hwang, "Media Literacy Interventions: A Meta-Analytic Review," *Journal of Communication* 62 (2012): 454–72. doi: 10.1111/j.1460-2466.2012.01643.x. See also Lynda J. Bergsma and Mary E. Carney, "The Effec-

tiveness of Health-Promoting Media Literacy Education: A Systematic Review," *Health Education Research* 23, (2008): 522–42.

24. National Institute of Mental Health (NIMH), *The Teen Brain: Still under Construction*. Bethesda, MD: US Department of Health and Human Services, 2011, 4.

25. S. Shirley Feldman and Glen R. Elliott, eds., *At the Threshold: The Developing Adolescent*. Cambridge, MA: Harvard University Press, 1990.

26. Cornelia Pechmann, Linda Levine, Sandra Loughlin, and Frances Leslie, "Impulsive and Self-Conscious: Adolescents' Vulnerability to Advertising and Promotion," *Journal of Public Policy and Marketing* 24, no. 2 (2005): 202–21.

27. Laurence Steinberg, "Risk Taking in Adolescence: New Perspectives from Brain and Behavioral Science," *Current Directions in Psychological Science* 16, no. 2 (2007): 55–59.

28. Thomas Hine, *The Rise and Fall of the American Teenager*. New York: Harper Perennial, 2000, 11.

ONE

A Nation at Risk

The 2014 *Surgeon General's Vision for a Healthy and Fit Nation* admonishes Americans of all ages to reduce the consumption of sugary beverages; to eat more fruits, vegetables, whole grains, and lean proteins; to drink more water and choose low-fat or nonfat dairy products; and to limit television time to no more than two hours per day and to be more physically active. This vision has yet to be realized, however. This chapter explores the current data relative to the health challenges of Americans and in particular the population of adolescent youth (ages twelve to nineteen). The escalation of obesity at a global level in particular and the lack of clear solutions signal a larger set of social, economic, and political issues that converge to shape public health in ways that are opaque and even perplexing—especially for one of the most powerful nations in the world.

A STATISTICAL SNAPSHOT

A statistical snapshot of public health in the United States reveals a disturbing portrait of a nation of sleep-deprived, unhappy people with insatiable and even dangerous appetites for sugary beverages, prescription drugs, junk food, and sedentary lifestyles dominated by cars and screen-based technologies. While the data presented here provide neither a clear nor nuanced picture, they are worth exploring as they both directly and indirectly inform policy and decision making in the United States.

An Obsession with Sugar and Caffeine

Despite the recommendation of the surgeon general for individuals of all ages to reduce the consumption of sodas and juices with added sugars, Americans consume twenty teaspoons of added sugars a day, or twice the recommended amount. Sugary beverages (including soda, juices, and juice drinks) comprise the greatest source of added sugars in the American diet.[1] Sugary beverages are the number one source of calories in the diet of teenagers.[2] Approximately 40 percent of added sugars in teens' diets come from soda,[3] and one high school student out of every four drinks soda every day.[4] Our obsession with sugar is not surprising in light of recent research concluding that refined sugar like that contained in soda beverages is physiologically more addictive than cocaine.[5, 6]

Excessive intake of sugar leads to a blood sugar roller coaster-like effect of high energy followed by fatigue, which, among other things, can negatively impact sleep. Nearly 30 percent of adults in the United States report an average of less than six hours of sleep per night, or one to two hours below the recommended level.[7] Only 31 percent of high school students report getting the recommended eight and a half to nine hours of sleep on an average school night.[8]

To compensate for lack of sleep, Americans rely on caffeine and stimulants. The United States is the leading consumer of coffee in the world with 83 percent of adults drinking coffee and 63 percent drinking it on a daily basis.[9] While fewer teens than adults consume coffee, caffeine consumption among teens is mainly through energy drinks and soft drinks. Desperate to stay focused and energized in order to excel academically, high school and college students use "study drugs" at great expense to their physical and emotional well-being.[10]

Prescription Drug Use

About half of the U.S. population is currently taking some sort of prescription drug.[11] The use of antidepressants, particularly among teenagers and children, has dramatically increased over the past two decades. One out of every twenty-five teenagers takes antidepressant drugs on a regular basis, and the usage is often long term. Teens especially fall into the false assumption that prescription drugs are safer than illicit drugs since they are prescribed by a healthcare professional and dispensed by a pharmacist.[12] Not only does this self-medication impact the self-identity development of adolescents, it also reframes mental illness as exclusively a medical (physiological) problem and even risks emotional illiteracy among teenagers.[13]

The abuse of prescription drugs is rampant in the United States and prescription drug overdoses are now more deadly than motor vehicle collisions.[14] In 2011, there were more deaths among the entire U.S. population from prescription painkiller overdoses than there were from both heroin and cocaine combined.[15] Accidental poisoning deaths (primarily through prescription painkillers) among teens increased 91 percent from

2000 to 2009, raising serious concern at the Centers for Disease Control and Prevention (CDCP).[16] It is also significant that the United States is one of only two countries in the world that has legalized the broadcasting of drug commercials.

A Complicated Relationship with Food

A confluence of changes over the past eighty years compels Americans to eat food away from home instead of preparing and eating it at home.[17] These catalysts include women entering the workforce, technological innovation both inside and outside the food industry, the growth of advertising, and the industrialization of the food industry making low-cost foods affordable to consumers. Mass media are saturated with messages about food, yet we spend only thirty minutes a day actually preparing food.[18] In American culture, mothers used to be the primary source of cooking instruction yet are now replaced by cookbooks and cooking shows.[19]

Between 1977 and 1995, Americans tripled their time spent eating at fast-food restaurants and quadrupled their percentage of daily caloric intake from fast food.[20] In 1929, 17 percent of all food expenditures were made on foods away from home as compared to 49 percent in 2011.[21] While there was a slight decrease in fast-food consumption from 2006 to 2010, Americans still consume on average more than 10 percent of their daily calories from fast food. Teenagers consume the largest portion of calories away from home at fast-food restaurants.[22] When it comes to food selection outside the home, Americans favor taste and cost over nutritional value.[23] The Center for Science in the Public Interest (CSPI) recently reported that 97 percent of kids' meals at top U.S. restaurant chains do not meet United States Department of Agriculture (USDA) nutritional standards.[24] Social science research finds that eating away from home is exciting[25] and considered a mainstream way to socialize in the United States.[26] At the same time, medical experts suggest that relying less on restaurants and learning how to cook at home will significantly contribute to reducing obesity.[27]

Americans may choose convenience over nutrition, but this does not diminish the fact that existing corporate structures make nutrition an inconvenience or in some cases inaccessible. The USDA estimates that more than 116 million Americans live in "food deserts," where there is no affordable, easy access to supermarkets.[28] Instead, sugary, low nutritive foods such as soda, cookies, and donuts are more easily accessible and affordable than high nutrition foods. Even outside of food deserts, the choices are highly limited by external forces, and the idea of food "choice" is highly illusory. In *Stuffed and Starved*, global activist Raj Patel sums up the global imbalance in our food ecology: There are more people starving in the world than ever before while there are also more people overweight than ever before. He writes: "most of what we consider our choices at the consumer end of the food system have been narrowed and shaped before we even begin to think consciously about them."[29] Food activists such as Michael Pollan, Melanie Warner, and Raj Patel call attention to the deep and broad imbalance and even conflict that exists between nutrition and convenience.[30]

Fast-food marketers especially target minority groups in an effort to increase sales. A 2013 study by the Yale Rudd Center for Food Policy and Obesity found that black teens saw 80 to 90 percent more ads for sugary drinks than their white peers, and Latino teens were exposed to 99 percent more ads in 2010 than they were in 2008.[31] More junk food ads appear in Spanish TV programming for youth than the same type of programs in English. Less than 1 percent of Spanish TV programming for youth contains ads that promoted fruits, vegetables, whole grains, or other healthy foods.[32]

A Sedentary and Technologized Culture

The United States has transitioned into a sedentary culture since the Industrial Revolution of the early nineteenth century. Increases in desk jobs, automobile and highway transportation, neighborhood violence, reduced time spent on physical education in schools, increase in leisure time, and the proliferation of screen-based technologies (e.g., TV, computer, smart phones) are just a few of the factors contributing to sedentary lifestyles.[33] Between 25 and 35 percent of American adults are considered "inactive," meaning sedentary employment, no regular physical activity, and generally inactive at home.[34, 35] Between 1969 and 2001, the percentage of high school students walking or biking to school decreased from 26 percent to 8 percent.[36] When it comes to the physical activity of teenagers, only 29 percent of high school students participate in sixty or more minutes a day of physical activity, according to a 2012 government survey.[37] Around 14 percent of high school students are not participating in *any* type of physical activity on any day during a seven-day period. Girls are less likely (at 19 percent) than boys (at 38 percent) to engage in sixty or more minutes a day of physical activity.

In the early 1990s Bill McKibbin wrote *The Age of Missing Information* to juxtapose the confusion and artificiality of the TV viewing experience with the sheer sensory joy of being outdoors. Twenty years later, fewer children climb trees or enjoy the outdoors and instead watch programs like *Survivor* and *The Biggest Loser* from the comfort of their couch. Teens watch on average three hours and twenty-one minutes of TV per day.[38] A 2012 Children's Hospital National Poll on Children's Health found the number one concern among Caucasian adults is that children get insufficient exercise—a concern ranked even higher than childhood obesity, smoking, drug use, bullying, stress, alcohol abuse, teen pregnancy, Internet safety, child abuse, and neglect.[39] Mary Collins notes in *American Idle* that "simply bringing [children] into the woods is no longer enough; parents and educators must now deliberately teach children how to be *in* nature."[40] Being physically active and engaging in the physical world requires effort and intentionality.

Young people are learning about the world through devices and screens and less through direct lived experience. In 2010, children (ages eight to eighteen) spent more than seven hours a day with digital media, including TV, computers, and video games.[41] Not surprisingly, teens that lack positive relationships with their parents have a higher frequency of Internet use.[42] A recent report by the Joan Ganz Cooney Center indicates about 59 percent of parents believe that digital media prevent children from getting physical exercise, while 53 percent are concerned about their children's online safety and privacy. Forty percent believe that mediated activities infringe on time that would otherwise be spent in face-to-face interactions. Only 18 percent of parents indicate that their own children spend too much time with technology.[43] While parents are concerned about their children's inactivity, the motivation may be more social (stigmas associated with isolation, overweight, and obesity) than about the actual physiological benefits of increased physical activity.

A nation at war with itself is not merely a metaphor in this case. According to the CDCP, homicide remains a leading cause of death among young people ages ten to twenty-four in the United States, and violence is a major cause of nonfatal injuries among young people.[44] It is no longer uncommon to see news reports of enraged teenagers instigating school shootings, suggesting a widespread inability for teenagers to dissent in ways that are safe and civil. There is an increasing need for coping mechanisms that are conducive to emotional and mental health rather than destructive to life.

These are just a few of the data strands woven into the fabric of American culture in 2014. There are certainly other major strands that require much deeper and more intricate discussions (including mental health and sexual behavior) that this space and my expertise will allow. However, within this delimited space a portrait emerges of a nation engaged in an internal struggle. As individuals, we have ultimate stewardship and accountability over our physical body, but the power of institutional forces muddies our intellectual ability to choose. The public health threats associated with sugary beverages, fast food, prescription drugs, and physical inactivity comprise what some cultural critics call an "industrial epidemic" where corporations undermine public health through complex media campaigns and the strategic shaping of public policy.[45]

The war is fought between the democratic ideal of individual choice and accountability and the powerful capitalistic, free-market economy that privileges—even demands—efficiency, productivity, and consumerism—often at the expense of public health.[46] One particular battle that doesn't seem to have a resolution on the horizon is obesity. Two major weapons wielded in this proverbial war are confusion and obscurity, both of which pervade the discourse about obesity.

THE CONUNDRUM OF OBESITY

Obesity has been referred to as an epidemic, a disease, and most recently a worldwide pandemic. The World Health Organization (WHO) identifies obesity as the most significant unrecognized public health problem today.[47] Obesity is technically calculated according to body mass index (BMI), also known as the Quetelet Index, created in 1832 by the Belgian astronomer and statistician Adolphe Quetelet.[48] The BMI index was originally based on data from the French and Scottish armies. Quetelet divided a soldier's weight by the square of his height and found that most bodies fell within that range.[49] Overweight is considered to be a BMI calculation of at least twenty-five and obesity is a BMI of thirty or higher. BMI is a flawed measure on multiple levels: It does not measure body type, fat percentage, cardiovascular health, or overall fitness. Moreover, females may actually be fatter or less fat than their BMI indicates.[50] These and other limitations raise serious doubt concerning the BMI as a valid measurement of obesity.[51]

Despite the questionable validity of BMI, it remains the current standard measure for overweight and obesity. Based on BMI, more than 35 percent of adults in the United States are currently obese,[52] and 69.4 percent of the entire U.S. population is either overweight or obese.[53] The obesity rate has risen steadily in the United States over the past 150 years, but has seen a dramatic increase over the past twenty years.[54] In 1999, the U.S. Department of Health officially declared obesity to be an epidemic.[55] Obesity is considered a major cause of death by heart disease, cancer, and diabetes. One out of three people born in the United States today will develop Type II diabetes over his or her lifetime. Data show that severely obese people die eight to ten years sooner than those of normal weight — a death rate similar to that of smokers. A person's risk of early death increases by approximately 30 percent for every thirty-three pounds (fifteen extra kilograms) of weight.[56] For these and other reasons, the American Medical Association in 2013 classified obesity as a disease.

The United States is known as an "obesigenic" culture. The country accounts for almost a third of the world's weight yet comprises only 5 percent of the world's population.[57] Until 2013, the United States was known for the highest obesity rate of any developed nation.[58] Mexico now surpasses the United States with an obesity rate of 32.8 percent.[59] The Americas are not alone, however. According to the WHO, obesity is a global epidemic that has doubled its worldwide growth rate since 1980.[60] In the twenty-seven member states comprising the European Union (EU), approximately 60 percent of adults are overweight or obese.[61] In 2008, the WHO reported twenty-three countries with higher obesity rates than the United States. The seven most obese countries in the world are located in the South Pacific, with the island country Nauru ranking the highest at 71 percent obesity, more than double the rate in the United States.[62] These data support the classification of obesity as a global pandemic.

Childhood obesity is said to have reached pandemic proportions.[63] Approximately 17 percent of children and adolescents (ages two to eighteen) in the United States are obese.[64] One out of every six adolescents is overweight, and one out of every three is at risk for becoming overweight.[65] Currently, more than a quarter of seventeen- to twenty-four-year-olds are considered unfit to enroll in the U.S. military due to their weight.[66] In the EU, 20 percent of children are overweight or obese[67] and the number of overweight children in the EU is increasing by more than four hundred thousand per year.[68] Two-thirds of the people fifteen years and older in the EU are not physically active at recommended levels, and only one-third of the schoolchildren meet recognized physical activity guidelines. [69, 70]

The consequences of childhood obesity are thought to be debilitating and even deadly, as obese children are more likely to become obese adults.[71,72] Childhood obesity has also recently been linked to increased risk for blindness.[73] The potential consequences of childhood obesity are considered a greater threat than the use of tobacco, drugs, and alcohol combined.[74] In fact, young people today may even be the first generation of Americans with a shorter average life span than their parents.

Many parents of overweight or obese children do not recognize their child's weight problem,[75] and only 10 percent of parents of obese children seek professional help for them.[76] Pediatricians are more likely to advise obese boys and girls about healthy eating habits and exercise than they are to advise children at a normal weight. This is paradoxical in that obesity is easier to prevent than to treat.[77] Obese children are more likely than normal weight children to report poorer health; more disability; more emotional and behavioral problems; depression; learning disabilities; developmental delays; bone, joint, and muscle problems; asthma; allergies; headaches; ear infections; higher number of missed school days; and higher rates of grade repetition.[78] Parents who try to help their children overcome obesity face an uphill battle and even criticism. Dara-Lynn Weis, parent and author of *The Heavy: A Mother, A Daughter, A Diet—A Memoir*, writes about her experiences parenting an obese child and calls attention to the overwhelming opposition and judgment in the surrounding environment and unpopularity of making strict decisions.[79]

What remains unclear and requires further study is the degree to which the conditions listed above are causes and which are effects of obesity. While the research tends to link obesity with poor academic performance in children,[80] the reality is that socioeconomic status more

so than obesity is a more reliable determinant of poor academic performance.[81] To what degree is obesity a cause and/or effect of physiological,
sociological, and/or economic conditions? The literature is unclear as to
which came first—obesity itself or its associated health risks.

Obesity: Cause, Effect, or Both?

Obesity was once thought to be a favorable sign of eighteenth-century
technological advances that afforded gradual increases in the food supply. In the nineteenth century, however, aesthetics and health liabilities
led to the stigmatization of obesity. Post–WWI data revealed a third of
drafted personnel to be unfit for combat, thus triggering government
legislation to promote physical education in schools. The U.S. government also began subsidizing farms prior to the Great Depression, thus
reducing the price of food (especially corn). Over the course of a century
the number of calories available to the average American ultimately grew
by about one thousand per day. In response to increased mortality rates
in the second half of the twentieth century, the insurance industry fully
condemned obesity.[82]

Understanding obesity depends upon one's disciplinary perspective,
and even across disciplines there is variance. From a mathematical standpoint, obesity is a result of overproduction of food and an excess of
calories consumed versus calories expended.[83,84] Traditional medical
wisdom attributed obesity to gluttony and sloth, yet some medical researchers argue that obesity is less about an energy imbalance and more
about a hormonal defect.[85,86] Some medical experts reframe obesity as a
systemic disease, of which food consumption is merely one component.[87]
Others are interested in the idea that chemicals in the environment could
be contributing to obesity.[88] In 2011 the National Institute of Health
(NIH) launched a three-year study exploring the role of environmental
chemical exposures in obesity, Type II diabetes, and metabolic syndrome.[89] Other medical researchers point to the possibility that food additives including food colorings, preservatives, artificial sweeteners, iron,
an emulsifier common in dairy products, and even food packaging may
be contributing to obesity.[90]

Other researchers similarly suggest that some of the physical and
mental health effects of the obesity pandemic are related to the way we
perceive our bodies, through a lens that is socially constructed.[91] Julie
Guthman, a social scientist at University of California Santa Cruz, asserts
that the "obesity-disease connection has been established by reductive
measurements, correlative reasoning rather than causal determination,
and rhetorical devices that leave out as much as they tell."[92]

Even more dangerous is the extent to which our scientific lenses are
clouded. False and scientifically unsupported beliefs about obesity pervade the popular press as well as the scientific literature. A recent study

published in the *New England Journal of Medicine* identified obesity myths as "Snacking contributes to weight gain and obesity" and obesity facts as "Some pharmaceutical agents can help patients achieve clinically meaningful weight loss."[93] While these statements may contain a degree of truth, one cannot ignore the fact that the study was funded by the pharmaceutical industries, which renders the findings highly suspect in terms of their scientific validity and social implications.

There are also others that focus on the media messages that are indirect yet powerful promoters of obesity. Open source guru Clay Johnson asserts in the *Information Diet* that "obesity isn't caused simply by cheap access to food, but in part by an abundance of cheap and often misleading information about food . . . information obesity can cause actual obesity."[94] He argues that unhealthy information diets are similar to unhealthy food addictions. Knowing what information to consume and what information to avoid is not a luxury but rather mandatory to our survival. Along a similar vein, Brooks Richey in *Does This News Make Me Look Fat?* warns media consumers that we can too easily develop mental obesity through consuming junk media that renders us mentally out of shape and intellectually lazy.[95]

There is also a growing trend of citizen journalists calling into question scientific truths once thought to be valid. Documentary films such as *Fathead* (2009) and *Cereal Killers* (2013) take the audience on the filmmakers' personal journeys through a high protein/high fat diet to seemingly beneficial results. By doing so the documentaries disrupt traditional science by refuting the lipid fat theory linking cholesterol levels to heart disease.

Socioeconomic Disparities of Obesity

There is a clear inverse relationship in most societies between the level of education or socioeconomic status and the prevalence of obesity.[96] Like many other public health problems, overweight and obesity have disproportionate impacts on disadvantaged communities and racial and ethnic minorities. Nine of the ten states with the highest obesity prevalence are also among the poorest. It is therefore no coincidence that the state of Mississippi has both the highest obesity rate and also the highest percentage of people living in poverty. Obesity also affects poor children disproportionately. Twenty percent of low-income children are obese, compared with about 12 percent of children from more affluent families.[97] Surprisingly, however, the obesity rate among the homeless is equal to that of the general population.[98] This may be due to reliance on cheap foods that contain high levels of fat and sugar. Other possible explanations are physiological: chronic food shortages may cause the body to adapt by storing fat reserves; too little physical activity; sleep deprivation; and even stress.

Overweight and obesity disproportionately affect Hispanics and African Americans. The CDCP data show that 72 percent of Hispanics, 84 percent of African Americans, and 68 percent of non-Hispanic whites are overweight or obese.[99] In order to meet the federal goals for obesity reduction by 2020, black children and adolescents (ages two to nineteen) will need to reduce caloric intake by 138 calories a day, Hispanic by 91 fewer calories, and white children by 46 fewer calories.[100] Obesity is also economically stratified along gender lines. Less-educated women are two to three times more likely than their educated counterparts to be overweight, suggesting the need for educational interventions that target specific at-risk groups based on race, class, and gender.

The failure to reduce the obesity pandemic in any measurable way is curious given the wealth and technological power of the U.S. economy as compared to other nations'.[101] From a fiscal standpoint, obesity reportedly costs the United States $150 billion annually, or 10 percent of the national medical budget.[102] Treatment for obesity-related conditions accounts for 27 percent of the rise in healthcare costs over the past twenty years,[103] and that number is projected to double to US$300 billion by 2030.[104] The United States spends five times more on health care than on the defense budget.[105] According to the CDCP, the amount of money lost annually as a result of women being obese is nearly double that of men.[106] Obese female workers earn up to 18 percent less than nonobese workers.[107] Ironically, even a billion-dollar corporation like Coca-Cola, Inc. relies on the health of its more than 92,000 employees and their families.

It is also difficult to ignore the profitable weight loss industry that both fuels and is perpetuated by the obesity pandemic. At any given moment, one-third of the U.S. population is on a weight loss diet. In 2012, the annual revenue of the U.S. weight loss industry (including diet books, diet drugs, and weight loss surgeries) reached US$20 billion. Medical and commercial weight loss programs, diet drugs, diet foods, and retail diet products together are worth about US$12 billion a year.[108] Currently, seventy-five million Americans are on a diet, and 80 percent of dieters try to lose weight on their own without joining a group or seeing a registered dietician. In 2009, the total revenue generated by online dieting was estimated at $842 million.[109] In 2010, Weight Watchers revenue for online only memberships was $238 million.[110] Despite these figures, most people who participate in a restrictive weight loss program regain about one-third of the weight lost and are back to their baseline weight in three to five years.[111]

Research also indicates that most diet fads rotate in and out of popularity, and many techniques may even be hazardous to one's health.[112] Despite the relatively low success rate for dieters, the weight loss industry shows no signs of decline. The commercial trend is for smaller weight loss clinics to appear in supermarkets and retailers such as Walmart or in shopping mall kiosks.[113] This retail approach packaged as individualized but sold en masse perpetuates the concept that it is the lone responsibility of the consumer to press forward in the uphill battle against overweight and obesity.

In sum, there is no singular solution to addressing the pandemic of obesity. Although recent data suggest that childhood obesity rates are plateauing for young children in the United States, there remains much that health professionals do not understand about obesity, despite it being a preventable disease. Framing it solely in terms of economics marginalizes at-risk groups according to the extent to which they are perceived as burdensome to the national healthcare system. There is also danger in looking at health or obesity primarily through the clinical lens of medicine as it situates individuals as patients, consumers, or worse—as disempowered victims.[114] Individuals are therefore faced with a highly complex definition of *obesity* that is no less than a myriad of genetic, biological, behavioral, cultural, social, and political factors.[115]

The Institute of Medicine rejects the idea that obesity is mainly caused by a lack of willpower and argues that multiple strategies—including those that food industry and lawmakers resist—are essential to slowing down the rate of obesity. The WHO suggests that healthcare policies and practices are more likely to be successful if they modify both the physical and social environments rather than simply rely on the limited success of changing individual behavior.[116] Addressing the obesity pandemic, for example, requires full participation and leadership of industry (including marketing practices) and a proactive approach to fostering healthy behaviors in children.[117] To shift the paradigm from treatment of illness to the proactive pursuit of health, all stakeholders need to be involved in this pursuit.

MOVING BEYOND THE DATA

To adults, the future of teenagers appears quite bleak. According to a 2013 poll, adults are highly pessimistic about the future of young people. The majority believe that teenagers will not have the same opportunities as they did when they were young—including less opportunity for a quality education, access to health care, fair treatment, adequate playtime, and sufficient love and attention.[118] The same poll, however, reveals that teenagers are optimistic about their future. Forty-five percent of teenagers polled believe they will have *more* opportunities than their parents had growing up. At the same time, youthful optimism without agency or action will be fruitless. The solutions may lie with the very population that adults are trying to protect: teenagers themselves and those who educate them.

The data presented in this chapter portray a nation, even a world, out of balance. The extent to which these data reflect the realities of individuals is contested, however, as those who control the modes of communication also have power over health messaging. I now switch gears to focus on health as a moral dilemma and less a scientific conundrum. In search of deeper insight, the next chapter examines the intersecting U.S. histories of media, technological development, and the emergence of adolescent youth culture.

NOTES

1. Rachel K. Johnson, Lawrence J. Appel, Michael Brands, Barbara V. Howard, Michael Lefevre, Robert H. Lustig, Frank Sacks, Lyn M. Steffen, and Judith Wylie-Rosett, "Dietary Sugars Intake and Cardiovascular Health: A Scientific Statement from the American Heart Association," *Circulation: Journal of the American Heart Association*, August 24, 2009, doi: 10.1161/CIRCULATIONAHA.109.192627.

2. Jill Reed and Susan M. Krebs-Smith, "Dietary Sources of Energy, Solid Fats, and Added Sugars among Children and Adolescents in the United States," *Journal of the American Dietetic Association* 110, no. 10 (October 2010): 1477–84, doi: 10.1016/j.jada.2010.07.010.

3. Joanne F. Guthrie and Joan F. Morton, "Food Sources of Added Sweeteners in the Diets of Americans," *Journal of the American Dietetic Association* 100, no. 1 (January 2000): 43–51, doi: 10.1016/S0002-8223(00)00018-3.

4. Centers for Disease Control and Prevention, *Obesity: Halting the Epidemic by Making Health Easier* (2011), http://www.cdc.gov/chronicdisease/resources/publications/aag/pdf/2011/Obesity_AAG_WEB_508.pdf.

5. Magalie Lenoir, Fuschia Serre, Lauriane Cantin, and Serge H. Ahmed, "Intense Sweetness Surpasses Cocaine Reward," *PLoS ONE* 2, no. 8 (2007): e698, doi: 10.1371/journal.pone.0000698.

6. Robert H. Lustig, *Fat Chance: Beating the Odds against Sugar, Processed Food, Obesity, and Disease*. New York: Hudson Street Press, 2012.

7. National Sleep Foundation, "How Much Sleep Do We Really Need?" (2013), http://www.sleepfoundation.org/article/how-sleep-works/how-much-sleep-do-we-really-need.

8. Centers for Disease Control, "Youth Risk Behavior Surveillance—United States, 2009," *MMWR* 59 (2010): SS–5.

9. National Coffee Association, "NCA Releases 2013 Coffee Consumption Data" [press release], March 22, 2013, http://www.ncausa.org/custom/headlines/headlinedetails.cfm?id=871&returnto=1.

10. Alan Schwartz, "In Their Own Words: Study Drugs," *New York Times*, June 9, 2012, http://www.nytimes.com/interactive/2012/06/10/education/stimulants-student-voices.html?ref=prescriptiondrugabuse&_r=0#/#1.

11. Centers for Disease Control National Center for Health Statistics, *Health, United States, 2012: With Special Feature on Emergency Care*. Hyattsville, MD: National Center for Health Statistics, 2013, 282 http://www.cdc.gov/nchs/data/hus/hus12.pdf#091.

12. The White House Office of National Drug Control Policy, "Prescription Drug Abuse," http://www.whitehouse.gov/ondcp/prescription-drug-abuse.

13. Katherine Sharp, "The Medication Generation," *Wall Street Journal*, June 29, 2012, http://online.wsj.com/articles/SB10001424052702303649504577493112618709108.

14. The White House Office of National Drug Control Policy, "Epidemic: Responding to America's Prescription Drug Abuse Crisis," (2011), http://www.whitehouse.gov/sites/default/files/ondcp/issues-content/prescription-drugs/rx_abuse_plan.pdf.

15. Margaret Warner, Li Hui Chen, Diane M. Makuc, Robert N. Anderson, and Arialdi M. Miniño, "Drug Poisoning Deaths in the United States, 1980–2008," *NCHS Data Brief, No. 81*. Hyattsville, MD: National Center for Health Statistics, 2011.

16. Centers for Disease Control and Prevention, "Vital Signs: Unintentional Injury Deaths among Persons Aged 0–19 Years—United States, 2000–2009" (Early Release, April 16, 2012): 1–7, http://www.cdc.gov/mmwr/preview/mmwrhtml/mm61e0416a1.htm?s_cid=mm61e0416a1_w.

17. Lisa M. Powell, Binh T. Nguyen, and Euna Han, "Energy Intake from Restaurants: Demographics and Socioeconomics, 2003–2008," *American Journal of Preventive Medicine* 43, no. 5 (November 2012): 498–504, http://dx.doi.org/10.1016/j.amepre.2012.07.041.

18. Lucia Moses, "A By-the-Numbers Look at Consumers' Complex Relationship with Food," *Data Points: How We Eat*, August 8, 2012, http://www.adweek.com/news/advertising-branding/data-points-how-we-eat-142531.

19. Joanne F. Guthrie, Biing-Hwan Lin, and Elizabeth Frazao, "Role of Food Prepared Away from Home in the American Diet, 1977–78 versus 1994–96: Changes and Consequences," *Journal of Nutrition Education and Behavior* 34, no. 2 (2002): 140–50.

20. Guthrie, Lin, and Frazao, "Role of Food Prepared Away from Home in the American Diet."

21. United States Department of Agriculture Economic Research Service, "Food away from Home as a Share of Food Expenditures," 2011, http://www.ers.usda.gov/data-products/food-expenditures.aspx.

22. Samara Joy Nielsen, Anna Maria Siega-Riz, and Barry M. Popkin, "Trends in Food Locations and Sources among Adolescents and Young Adults," *Preventative Medicine* 35, no. 2 (2002): 107–13, doi: 10.1006/pmed.2002.1037.

23. Karen Glanz, Michael Basil, Edward Maibach, Jeanne Goldberg, and Dan Snyder, "Why Americans Eat What They Do: Taste, Nutrition, Cost, Convenience, and Weight Control Concerns as Influences on Food Consumption," *Journal of the American Dietetic Association* 98, no. 10 (1998): 1118–26, doi: 10.1016/S0002-8223(98)00260-0.

24. Ameena Batada, "Kids' Meals II: Obesity and Poor Nutrition on the Menu," *Center for Science in the Public Interest*, March 2013, http://cspinet.org/new/pdf/cspi-kids-meals-2013.pdf.

25. Hayden Stewart, Noel Blisard, and Dean Jolliffe, "Let's Eat Out: Americans Weigh Taste, Convenience, and Nutrition," *Economic Information Bulletin* 19 (October 2006).

26. Alan Warde and Lydia Martens, *Eating Out*. New York: Cambridge University Press, 2000.

27. Yoni Freedhoff, "Opinion: Why Does the American Heart Association Want You to Eat Out?" *US News & World Report*, July 11, 2012, http://health.usnews.com/health-news/blogs/eat-run/2012/07/11/opinion-why-does-the-american-heart-association-want-you-to-eat-out.

28. Michele Ver Ploeg, Vince Breneman, Tracey Farrigan, Karen Hamrick, David Hopkins, Phil Kaufman, Biing-Hwan Lin, Mark Nord, Travis Smith, Ryan Williams, Kelly Kinnison, Carol Olander, Anita Singh, and Elizabeth Tuckermanty, *Access to Affordable and Nutritious Food—Measuring and Understanding Food Deserts and Their Consequences: Report to Congress*, Ap-036. Washington, DC: Economic Research Service, U.S. Department of Agriculture, 2009.

29. Raj Patel, *Stuffed and Starved: The Hidden Battle for the World Food System*. New York: Melville House, 2007, 254–55.

30. Patel, *Stuffed and Starved*. See also Michael Pollan, *The Omnivore's Dilemma: A Natural History of Four Meals*. New York: Penguin Press, 2006; Melanie Warner, *Pandora's Lunchbox: How Processed Food Took Over the American Meal*. New York: Scribner, 2013, 59.

31. Sugary Drink: Food Advertising to Children and Teens Score, *Sugary Drink Facts in Brief*. Robert Wood Johnson Foundation and the Rudd Foundation, 2013, http://www.sugarydrinkfacts.org/sugary_drink_facts_in_brief.aspx.

32. Dale Kunkel, Dana Mastro, Michelle Ortiz, and Christopher McKinley, "Food Marketing to Children on U.S. Spanish-Language Television," *Journal of Health Communication: International Perspectives*, doi: 10.1080/10810730.2013.768732.

33. Mary Collins, *American Idle: A Journey through Our Sedentary Culture*. Sterling, VA: Capital Books, Inc., 2009.

34. Mariane Héroux, Ian Janssen, Miu Lam, Duck-chul Lee, James R. Hebert, Xuemei Sui, and Steven N. Blair. "Dietary Patterns and the Risk of Mortality: Impact of Cardiorespiratory Fitness," *International Journal of Epidemiology* 39, no. 1 (February 2010): 197–209, doi: 10.1093/ije/dyp191.

35. In some southern states and Appalachia, the percentage of adults who are physically inactive is greater than 30 percent. See Centers for Disease Control and Prevention, "County Level Estimates of Leisure-time Physical Inactivity Among Adults Aged ≥ 20 Years," 2009, http://www.cdc.gov/diabetes/atlas/countydata/LTPIA%20Prevalence.pdf.

36. Noreen C. McDonald, "Active Transportation to School: Trends among U.S. Schoolchildren, 1969–2001," *American Journal of Preventive Medicine* 32, no. 6 (2007): 509–16.

37. U.S. Department of Health and Human Services, "Physical Activity Guidelines for Americans Midcourse Report Strategies to Increase Physical Activity among Youth," http://www.health.gov/paguidelines/midcourse/pag-mid-course-report-final.pdf, 2012.

38. Todd Juenger, "Why the Internet Won't Kill TV." Sanford C. Bernstein & Co.

39. C. S. Mott Children's Hospital, "Top 10 Child Health Concerns: Exercise, Obesity and Smoking Lead List," *National Poll on Children's Health* 16, no. 3 (August 20, 2012), http://mottnpch.org/sites/default/files/documents/082012Top10report.pdf.

40. Collins, *American Idle*, xxvi.

41. Victoria J. Rideout, Ulla G. Foehr, and Donald F. Roberts, *Generation M2: Media in the Lives of 8- to 18-Year-Olds: A Kaiser Family Foundation Study*. Menlo Park, CA: Kaiser Family Foundation, January 2010, http://www.kff.org/entmedia/upload/8010.pdf.

42. Teena Willoughby, "A Short-Term Longitudinal Study of Internet and Computer Game Use by Adolescent Boys and Girls: Prevalance, Frequency of Use, and Psychosocial Predictors," *Developmental Psychology* 44, no. 1 (2008): 195–2004.

43. Lori Takeuchi, "Families Matter: Designing Media for a Digital Age," *Joan Ganz Cooney Center at Sesame Workshop*, June 2011, http://www.joanganzcooneycenter.org/publication/families-matter-designing-media-for-a-digital-age/.

44. Centers for Disease Control and Prevention, "Youth Violence National and State Statistics at a Glance," 2013, http://www.cdc.gov/violenceprevention/youthviolence/stats_at-a_glance/.

45. Rob Moodie, David Stuckler, Carlos Monteiro, Nick Sheron, Bruce Neal, Thaksaphon Thamarangsi, Paul Lincoln, and Sally Casswell, "Profits and Pandemics: Prevention of Harmful Effects of Tobacco, Alcohol, and Ultra-Processed Food and Drink Industries," *Lancet* 381 (2013): 671.

46. Ben Agger, "The Dialectic of Deindustrialization: An Essay on Advanced Capitalism," in *Critical Theory and Public Life*, ed. J. Forrester, 3–21. Cambridge, MA: MIT Press, 1985.

47. Philip T. James, Rachel Leach, Eleni Kalamara, and Maryam Shayeghi, "The Worldwide Obesity Epidemic," *Obesity Research* 9 (2001): 228S–233S, doi: 10.1038/oby.2001.123.

48. Garabed Eknoyan, "Adolphe Quetelet (1796–1874)—The Average Man and Indices of Obesity," *Nephrology Dialysis Transplantation* 23 (2008): 47–51, doi: 10.1093/ndt/gfm517.

49. Garabed Eknoyan, "A History of Obesity, or How What Was Good Became Ugly and Then Bad," *Advances in Chronic Kidney Disease* 13, no. 4 (2006): 421–27, doi: 10.1053/j.ackd.2006.07.002.

50. Nirav R. Shah and Eric R. Braverman, "Measuring Adiposity in Patients: The Utility of Body Mass Index (BMI), Percent Body Fat, and Leptin," *PLOS ONE* 7, no. 4 (2012): e33308, doi: 10.1371/journal.pone.0033308.

51. Peter Janiszewski, "Why the Body Mass Index (BMI) Is a Poor Measure of Your Health," *PLOS* (blog), February 10, 2012, http://blogs.plos.org/obesitypanacea/2012/02/10/why-the-body-mass-index-bmi-is-a-poor-measure-of-your-health/.

52. Katherine M. Flegal, Margaret D. Carroll, Brian K. Kit, and Cynthia L. Ogden, JAMA. "Prevalence of Obesity and Trends in the Distribution of Body Mass Index among US Children and Adults," 1999–2010. http://dx.doi.org/10.1001/jama.2012.39.

53. World Health Organization, "Overweight and Obesity: Situation and Trends," 2008, http://gamapserver.who.int/gho/interactive_charts/ncd/risk_factors/overweight_obesity/atlas.html.

54. Dora L. Costa and Richard H. Steckel, "Long-Term Trends in Health, Welfare, and Economic Growth in the United States," in *Health and Welfare during Industrialization*, eds. Richard H. Steckel and R. Floud. (Chicago, IL: The University of Chicago Press, 1997) 47–90.

55. National Center for Biotechnology Information, "Obesity Declared an Epidemic in the United States," *Journal of the National Medical Association* 91, no. 12 (1999): 645, http://www.ncbi.nlm.nih.gov/pmc/articles/PMC2608606/pdf/jnma00357-0013b.pdf.

56. Organisation for Economic Co-operation and Development (OECD), "Obesity Update 2012," http://www.oecd.org/els/health-systems/49716427.pdf.

57. In comparison, Asia comprises 61 percent of the world's population but comprises only 13 percent of the world's weight. See Sarah Catherine Walpole, David Prieto-Merino, Phil Edwards, John Cleland, Gretchen Stevens, and Ian Roberts, "The Weight of Nations: An Estimation of Adult Human Biomass," *BMC Public Health* 12 (2012): 439, http://www.biomedcentral.com/1471-2458/12/439.

58. OECD, "Obesity Update 2012."

59. Food and Agriculture Organization of the United Nations, *The State of Food and Agriculture 2013* (Rome, 2013), http://www.fao.org/docrep/018/i3300e/i3300e.pdf.

60. WHO, "Obesity and Overweight: Fact Sheet No. 311," March 2013, http://www.who.int/mediacentre/factsheets/fs311/en/index.html.

61. WHO, "Obesity and Overweight."

62. WHO, "Obesity: Situation and Trends."

63. Simon Y. Sy Kimm and Eva E. Obarzanek, "Childhood Obesity: A New Pandemic of the New Millennium," *Pediatrics* 110, no. 5 (November 2002): 1003–7, doi: 10.1542/peds.110.5.1003.

64. Cynthia L. Ogden, Margaret D. Carroll, Brian K. Kit, and Katherine M. Flegal, "Prevalence of Obesity and Trends in Body Mass Index among US Children and Adolescents, 1999–2010," *Journal of the American Medical Association* 307, no. 5 (2012): 483–90, doi:10.1001/jama.2012.40.

65. Youfa Wang and May A. Beydoun, "The Obesity Epidemic in the United States Gender, Age, Socioeconomic, Racial/Ethnic, and Geographic Characteristics: A Systematic Review and Meta-Regression Analysis," *Epidemiologic Reviews* 29, no. 1 (2007): 6–28.

66. William Christeson, Amy Dawson Taggart, and Soren Messner-Zidell, *Too Fat to Fight: Retired Military Leaders Want Junk Food Out of America's Schools*. Washington, DC: Mission: Readiness, 2010, http://www.missionreadiness.org/wp-content/uploads/MR_Too_Fat_to_Fight-11.pdf.

67. WHO, "Obesity: Situation and Trends."

68. Tim Lobstein, Neville Rigby, and Rachel Leach, *International Obesity Task Force EU Platform Briefing Paper*. Brussels: International Obesity Task Force (IOTF) and European Association for the Study of Obesity, 2005, http://www.iotf.org/media/euobesity3.pdf.

69. Peggy Edwards and Agis Tsouros, "Promoting Physical Activity and Active Living in Urban Environments: The Role of Local Governments," Copenhagen, Den-

mark: World Health Organization Europe, 2006: 1, http://www.euro.who.int/__data/assets/pdf_file/0009/98424/E89498.pdf.

70. Candace Currie, Chris Roberts, Antony Morgan, Rebecca Smith, Wolfgang Settertobulte, Oddrun Samdal, and Vivian Barnekow Rasmussen, eds., "Young People's Health in Context. Health Behaviour in School-Aged Children (HBSC) Study: International Report from the 2001/2002 Survey," Health Policy for Children and Adolescents, no. 4. Copenhagen: WHO Regional Office for Europe, 2004, http://www.who.int/immunization/hpv/target/young-peoples-health-in-context_who_2011_2012.pdf.

71. Evelyn P. Whitlock, Selvi B. Williams, Rachel Gold, Paula R. Smith, and Scott A. Shipman, "Screening and Interventions for Childhood Overweight: A Summary of Evidence for the U.S. Preventive Services Task Force," *Pediatrics* 116, no. 1 (2005): e125–44.

72. Robert C. Whitaker, Jeffrey A. Wright, Margaret S. Pepe, Kristy D. Seidel, and William H. Dietz, "Predicting Obesity in Young Adulthood from Childhood and Parental Obesity," *New England Journal of Medicine* 37, no. 13 (1997): 869–73.

73. Sonu M. Brara, Corinna Koebnick, Amy H. Porter, and Annette Langer-Gould, "Pediatric Idiopathic Intracranial Hypertension and Extreme Childhood Obesity," *Journal of Pediatrics* 161, no. 4 (2012): 602–7, doi: 10.1016/j.jpeds.2012.03.047.

74. Susan Okie, *Fed Up! Winning the War against Childhood Obesity*. Dulles, VA: Joseph Henry Press, 2005.

75. Matthew D. Oettinger, Joanne P. Finkle, Denise Esserman, Lisa Whitehead, Thomas K. Spain, Steven R. Pattishall, Russell L. Rothman, and Eliana M. Perrin, "Color-Coding Improves Parental Understanding of Body Mass Index Charting," *Academic Pediatrics* 9, no. 5 (2009): 330–38, doi: 10.1016/j.acap.2009.05.028.

76. John Hoffman, Dan Chaykin, and Sarah Teale, 2012. *The Weight of the Nation*. [New York]: HBO Home Box Office, 2012, chapter 3, part I.

77. Lan Liang, Chad Meyerhoefer, and Justin Wang, "Obesity Counseling by Pediatric Health Professionals: An Assessment Using Nationally Representative Data," *Pediatrics* 131, no. 3 (2013): 894–902, doi: 10.1542/peds.2011-0596.

78. Neal Halfon, Kandyce Larson, and Wendy Slusser, "Associations between Obesity and Comorbid Mental Health, Developmental, and Physical Health Conditions in a Nationally Representative Sample of US Children Aged 10 to 17," *Academic Pediatrics* 13 (2013): 6–13.

79. Dara-Lynn Weiss, *The Heavy: A Mother, A Daughter, A Diet—A Memoir*. New York: Ballantine Books, 2013.

80. Sara Gable, Jennifer L. Krull, and Yiting Chang, "Boys' and Girls' Weight Status and Math Performance from Kindergarten Entry through Fifth Grade: A Mediated Analysis," *Child Development* 83, no. 5 (2012): 1822–39, doi: 10.1111/j.1467-8624.2012.01803.x.

81. Stephanie von Hinke Kessler Scholder, George Davey Smith, Debbie A. Lawlor, Carol Propper, and Frank Windmeijer, "Genetic Markers as Instrumental Variables: An Application to Child Fat Mass and Academic Achievement," Working Paper No. 10/229. Bristol, UK: Centre for Market and Public Organisation, January 2010, http://www.bristol.ac.uk/cmpo/publications/papers/2010/wp229.pdf.

82. Eknoyan, "A History of Obesity."

83. Carson Chow, "Dispelling the Myths of Obesity," presentation at the Annual Meeting of the American Association for the Advancement of Science (Vancouver, Canada, February 20, 2012).

84. Marion Nestle and Malden Nesheim, *Why Calories Count: From Science to Politics*. Berkeley: University of California Press, 2012.

85. Gary Taubes, *Good Calories, Bad Calories*. New York: Knopf, 2007.

86. Gary Taubes, *Why We Get Fat and What to Do about It*. New York: Knopf, 2010.

87. Robert H. Lustig, *Fat Chance: Beating the Odds against Sugar, Processed Food, Obesity, and Disease*. New York: Hudson Street Press, 2012.

88. Paula F. Baillie-Hamilton, "Chemical Toxins: A Hypothesis to Explain the Global Obesity Epidemic," *Journal of Alternative and Complementary Medicine* 8, no. 2 (2002):

185–92, http://dx.doi.org/10.1089/107555302317371479. See also Jeanett Louise Tang-Péronard, Henrik Rasmus Andersen, and B. L. Heitmann, "Endocrine-Disrupting Chemicals and Obesity Development in Humans: A Review," *Obesity Review* 12, no. 8 (2011): 622–36, http://dx.doi.org/10.1111/j.1467-789X.2011.00871.x.

89. National Institutes of Health (NIH), *Role of Environmental Chemical Exposures in the Development of Obesity, Type II Diabetes and Metabolic Syndrome* (R01), National Institutes of Health Grants [website], Bethesda, MD: National Institutes of Health, Department of Health and Human Services, 2011, http://grants.nih.gov/grants/guide/pa-files/PA-12-184.html.

90. Carey Goldberg, "What's Making Us Fat? Researchers Put Food Additives on Suspect List," *CommonHealth Reform and Reality*, August 12, 2011, http://commonhealth.wbur.org/2011/08/food-additives-obesity.

91. Peter Muennig, Haomiao Jia, Rufina Lee, and Erica Lubetkin, "I Think Therefore I Am: Perceived Ideal Weight as a Determinant of Health," *American Journal of Public Health* 98, no. 3 (2008): 501–6.

92. Julie Guthman, *Weighing In: Obesity, Food Justice, and the Limits of Capitalism*. Berkeley: University of California Press, 2011, 44.

93. Krista Casazza, Kevin R. Fontaine, Arne Astrup, Leann L. Birch, Andrew W. Brown, Michelle M. Bohan Brown, Nefertiti Durant, Gareth Dutton, Michael Foster, Steven Heymsfield, Kerry McIver, Tapan Mehta, Nir Menachemi, P. K. Newby, Russell Pate, Barbara J. Rolls, Bisakha Sen, Daniel L. Smith, Diana M. Thomas, and David B. Allison, "Myths, Presumptions, and Facts about Obesity," *New England Journal of Medicine* 368 (2013): 446–54. doi: 10.1056/NEJMsa1208051.

94. Clay A. Johnson, "Information Obesity and Food Obesity," *The Information Diet: A Case for Conscious Consumption* (blog), July 28, 2010, http://www.informationdiet.com/blog/read/information-obesity-and-food-obesity.

95. Brooks Richey, *Does This News Make Me Look Fat? America's Junk Food Media Diet Makes Us Mentally Obese. And the Diet Plan for Fitness*. Omena Publishing [e-book].

96. Philip T. James, Rachel Leach, Eleni Kalamara, and Maryam Shayeghi, "The Worldwide Obesity Epidemic," *Obesity Research* 9 (2001): 228S–233S, doi: 10.1038/oby.2001.123.

97. CDC, *Health, United States, 2012*.

98. Katherine A. Koh, Jessica S. Hoy, James J. O'Connell, and Paul Montgomery, "The Hunger-Obesity Paradox: Obesity in the Homeless," *Journal of Urban Health* 89, no. 6 (December 2012): 952–64, doi: 10.1007/s11524-012-9708-4.

99. PRWeb, "Weight Loss Market's Untapped Niches Could Add $2.4 Billion," September 27, 2012, http://www.prweb.com/releases/2012/9/prweb9948446.htm.

100. Y. Claire Wang, C. Tracy Orleans, and Steven L. Gortmaker, "Reaching the Healthy People Goals for Reducing Childhood Obesity: Closing the Energy Gap," *American Journal of Preventative Medicine* 42, no. 5 (2012): 437–44, doi: 10.1016/j.amepre.2012.01.018.

101. The World Bank Group, "United States," *The World Bank*, http://data.worldbank.org/indicator/NY.GDP.MKTP.CD.

102. National Center for Chronic Disease Prevention and Health Promotion, Division of Nutrition, Physical Activity and Obesity, "The Obesity Epidemic" [video], July 22, 2011, http://www.cdc.gov/CDCTV/ObesityEpidemic/.

103. Yale Rudd Center for Food Policy and Obesity, "Frequently Asked Questions," http://www. yaleruddcenter.org/what_we_do.aspx?id=79.

104. Hoffman, Chaykin, and Teale, *The Weight of the Nation*, chapter 4.

105. Hoffman, Chaykin, and Teal, *The Weight of the Nation*, chapter 4.

106. National Public Radio, "Obesity in America, by the Numbers," May 19, 2011, http://www.npr.org/2011/05/19/135601363/living-large-obesity-in-america.

107. OECD, "Obesity Update 2012."

108. PRWeb, "Weight Loss Market's Untapped Niches."

109. Tracey Sandilands, "The Financial Side of the Weight Loss Industry," *Houston Chronicle*, 2013, http://smallbusiness.chron.com/financial-side-weight-loss-industry-38200.html.

110. Sandilands, "The Financial Side of the Weight Loss Industry."

111. Rena R. Wing, Deborah F. Tate, Amy A. Gorin, Hollie A. Raynor, and Joseph L. Fava, "A Self-Regulation Program for Maintenance of Weight Loss," *New England Journal of Medicine*, October 12, 2006, doi: 355:1563-1571.

112. Wayne C. Miller, "How Effective Are Traditional Dietary and Exercise Interventions for Weight Loss?" *Medicine and Science in Sports and Exercise* 31, no. 8 (1999): 1129–34.

113. PRWeb, "Weight Loss Market's Untapped Niches."

114. Kathleen LeBesco, *Revolting Bodies? The Struggle to Redefine Fat Identity.* Amherst: University of Massachusetts, 2004.

115. American Academy of Child and Adolescent Psychiatry, "Obesity in Children and Teens," Facts for Families [fact sheet] No. 79 (March 2011), http://www.aacap.org/galleries/FactsForFamilies/79_obesity_in_children_and_teens.pdf.

116. Edwards and Tsouros, "Promoting Physical Activity and Active Living in Urban Environments."

117. J. Michael McGinnis, "Marketing, Leadership, and the Health of Children," *Archives of Pediatric and Adolescent Medicine* 164, no. 9 (2010): 878–79, doi: 10.1001/archpediatrics.2010.152.

118. Allstate/National Journal Heartland Monitor Poll, September 20, 2013.

TWO

A Social History of Media and Health

The emergence of each new media technology over time has created solutions to health problems yet has also created stumbling blocks to positive health behaviors. By understanding the connection between mass media, public health, and the social construction of adolescent youth culture we can better understand the possibilities for health education. To this end, this chapter highlights the historical epochs of print and broadcast media with particular attention to their impact on public health and education.

THE MORAL EPOCH OF PRINT

More than any other technological invention, the moveable type printing press revolutionized modern American life. The print era created a cadre of gatekeepers in the form of authors and publishers who determined what was worthy to publish and therefore what circulated throughout the public consciousness. Print ultimately allowed for rapid mass dissemination of ideas and subsequently the spread of religion, literacy, and schooling in colonial America. The expansion of global trade routes also fueled economic development and the circulation of commercial goods. Advertising expanded, along with newspapers and magazines. Large single sheets of paper (broadsides) and smaller handbills were the media for early English settlers to advertise and distribute public health notices in New England.

As early as the 1700s, Reverend Cotton Mather promoted smallpox inoculation through pamphlets and personal appeals. Posters, newspapers, handbills, banners, sandwich boards, booklets, pamphlets, journals, and magazines served as mechanisms for advertising and public health notices. In the seventeenth and eighteenth centuries, literacy was primarily a means for religious worship (through mass production of the Bible) and not essential for economic prosperity. Literacy was a mechanism for morality, which was interconnected to one's physical health.

Morality was both a mechanism for and an outcome of positive health behaviors. Print media served as a way to inform and persuade the public to avoid or engage in certain (un)acceptable behaviors. A common belief of the time was that those who engaged in morally questionable behavior or who were culturally inferior, which included the poor, were more likely to get cholera. In the United States, cholera outbreaks began in the 1830s and continued throughout the early 1900s. Print served as a means to document, memorialize, and warn about such events.

Print was more than just a means of documentation, however. Visual illustrations ultimately allowed for data analysis and discovery. In London in 1854, physician John Snow used a dot map to visually illustrate data on the correlation of water source (e.g, bacteria-laden drinking water) to cholera cases, thus facilitating a major breakthrough in discovering the causes of cholera and ultimately how to prevent it. The importance of this use of visual media for analysis and discovery cannot be overstated, for it signaled a shift in public understanding of the cholera epidemic as a result of poor sanitation rather than as the result of immoral behavior.

The American belief of physical health and its deep connection to morality and temperance lingered in the nineteenth century. As a schoolteacher, physician, and educational reformer, William Alcott situated the human body as essentially a temple to worship rather than defile, as outlined in his 1839 book *The House I Live In; Or the Human Body: For the Use of Families and Schools*. Alcott also wrote extensively about school design and physical education for the *Annals of Education*. Congruent with the puritanism of the time, Alcott and others framed health as a matter of tempering physiological, social, and moral behaviors. In 1856, Alcott authored *The Physiology of Marriage* that warned of the dangers of courtship among young people. Together with Reverend Sylvester Graham, Alcott promoted a nutrition reform campaign based on vegetarianism and later known as veganism. They used pamphlets, magazines, and books to promote temperance through healthy eating—which included abstention from alcohol and tobacco. Together, Alcott and Graham formed the American Physiological Society in 1837. Despite the public criticism and even mockery of Graham and Alcott's rather zealous approach to nutrition and sexual purity, the vegan movement that he and others began in the 1850s would ultimately come to symbolize a social justice approach to health that has gained momentum in the twenty-first century.

The Health Costs of Industrialization

Industrialization in the late 1880s came at great expense in the United States. The hectic pace and emergent chaos associated with urbanized lifestyle and the rapid evolution of technology fostered, among other things, nervous exhaustion, also known as *neurasthenia*.[1] Its symptoms included (but were not limited to) mental and physical fatigue, sadness, and constipation. The paucity of doctors and medical knowledge combined with the explosion of advertising during the late 1700s created a fertile environment for patent medicine or health-promoting elixirs that rarely worked as promoted. The inventors concealed the ingredients of their products, which often contained alcohol, narcotics, and, in some cases, poisons. Since there did not yet exist federal regulation concerning safety and effectiveness of drugs, the market was wide open for charlatans or "snake oil" salesmen to sell ineffective products. Even "physician approved" medical advertising in the nineteenth century featured alcohol-based syrups guaranteed to soothe a teething child or to invigorate and restore health.

Patent medicines were highly profitable, and their sales dramatically increased following the American Civil War due to the widespread self-medication of wounded veterans. Dr. John Smith Pemberton was one such veteran who suffered chronic pain from a war injury. He was also a druggist searching for a medicinal cure for his morphine addiction. In the process he stumbled upon the formula for Coca-Cola in 1886. Although Coke was first marketed as a nerve tonic, it was later promoted for indigestion relief. Coca-Cola was just one of many hybrid patent medicines and fruit-flavored carbonated beverages that were sold as health tonics at drugstore counters.

Also during this time, the Horlick brothers invented a mixture of barley, wheat flour, and milk dried into powder form and sold it as a nutritional supplement for infants and the elderly. Mixed with ice cream, malted milk became a popular beverage during the period of Prohibition and was symbolic of the temperance movement. By 1903, malt shops, soda shops, and drugstore soda fountains served ice cream sodas, chocolate malteds, fountain colas, and milkshakes. The popular drugstore soda fountain later expanded its menu to include burgers and French fries, evolving into what is known today as the modern fast-food restaurant. Over time, this motif was repeated in shopping mall food courts and more recently school cafeterias where fast-food vendors compete for patrons.

Late nineteenth-century industrialization also begat processed foods such as sliced bread, canned soups, frozen vegetables, and breakfast cereals that in turn afforded convenience to the increased number of women entering the workforce. The mid-nineteenth-century economic boom also fueled the development of suburbs and a standard of living that included plumbing, refrigerators, and automobiles. For some, an auto-mobile was more important than indoor plumbing, food, and even new clothes.[2] Weekends and free time were spent driving, instead of walking or visiting nearby neighbors or relatives. For the emerging "flapper" teenage culture in the 1920s, the automobile signified a coming of age that included smoking, drinking alcohol, experimenting with sex, and favoring peers over family.[3] In the context of increased industrialization and commerce of the United States, the progression from childhood to adulthood became increasingly difficult—and some argued it contrib-uted to the adult societal view of the adolescent as marginalized.[4]

High Schools as Moral Centers

Industrialization coupled with the formation of child labor laws de-creased need for children in the workforce, and the focus shifted to for-malized and ultimately compulsory secondary education. High schools were established in the early 1900s to prepare an educated citizenry, a skilled workforce, and (as a by-product) a youth consumer culture. In an effort to Americanize immigrants, educators integrated messages about American hygiene, food, and clothing with language lessons. Sports and athletics such as basketball, football, and cheerleading were central to high school culture and seen as an alternative to the immorality associat-ed with the flapper style. Physical health equated with moral upright-ness.

The commodification of teenagers through product marketing was generally seen as socially acceptable and a sign of industrialization and progress. By the mid-1920s, *Scholastic* magazine in schools featured ad-vertisements for athletic shoes, class rings, and life insurance. By the 1930s, the advertisements had expanded to products promising to im-prove a student's social life. In *Teenagers: An American History* historian Grace Palladino writes:

> Planters Peanuts, for example, would deliver popularity; Fleisch-mann's yeast could clear up complexion problems that stood in the way of romance; even Postum, a grain beverage substitute for coffee, offered students a path to beauty and social acceptance through good health.[5]

Until the 1930s in the United States, most young people ages twelve to seventeen worked on farms, in factories, or at home. The emergence of high schools in the 1940s created a centerpiece for teenagers' social lives. By 1945, 51 percent of seventeen-year-olds were high school graduates (as compared to only 6 percent in 1900), and in response to the wider range of abilities, the U.S. Office of Education created "life adjustment education" to make schools relevant to the daily life of teenagers.[6] Using posters, overhead projectors, and the latest technologies, teachers taught practical lessons in family life, hygiene, and health.

By the 1940s and 1950s, fast-food restaurants provided another social space for teenagers to congregate, drink nonalcoholic beverages, and listen to rock 'n' roll on jukeboxes. The rapid industrialization of the United States, including the development of modern communications technologies during the twentieth century, coupled with the commodification of the teenager, cultivated an increasingly commercial media environment. High school brought with it the contradictory mechanisms of commercialization and moral protectionism.

PROTECTING YOUTH IN A BROADCAST ERA

The late nineteenth and early twentieth century inventions of motion pictures, radio, and television marked the electronic age and the era of broadcast communication. The evolution of each media form increased the power of reaching audiences on a mass scale. Like print, broadcast media allowed a select group of authors, producers, and distributors to disseminate one-way messages to the masses without the ability for the audience to immediately respond. The dynamic multimodal qualities of sound, text, and moving images (and eventually the combination of all three) brought increased powers of persuasion through emotions rather than logic.

The first commercial radio broadcast in the United States occurred around 1920. Although initially government regulated, radio operated primarily through commercial sponsorships. Food and drink manufacturers sponsored programs and used commercial breaks to promote pain relievers, chewing gum, beer, cigarettes, soup, cereal, toothpaste, watches, cars, and a host of other products. In 1924, a little less than 5 percent of U.S. households owned a radio, but by 1928 the number had grown to nearly 28 percent.[7] Listening to the radio was a communal activity that the entire family could experience together. Radio also emerged as a highly accessible medium to which even the poor had access.

President Roosevelt used radio for "fireside chats" to unite the nation during the Great Depression and World War II. At the same time, media researchers during the 1920s and 1930s quantitatively measured the hidden social messages covertly transmitted by radio and later, film.[8] Audiences themselves began to critically question the message itself, as well as the sender of the messages, and what those messages represented when laid against the realities of the time.[9] The broadcasting industry followed suit and in the 1930s adopted codes to control program content.

The first movie cameras were developed in the late 1880s and the Nickelodeon cinema in 1905. Movie theaters became popular in the 1920s as another gathering place for young people to spend their increased amount of leisure time when they were not in school. In 1922, 40 percent of adolescent youth went to the movies at least twice a week and 45 percent more than once each week.[10] Silent films taught personal hygiene and good health, particularly to address overcrowding and to prevent the spread of tuberculosis. The 1928 silent film *General Health Habits* juxtaposed footage of crowded inner-city tenements and polluted air with the expanse, fresh air, and water of the rural countryside. The film associated juvenile delinquency with inner-city life in dramatic contrast to wholesome recreation associated with rural life. The health recommendations were to open the windows at night (a practice believed to combat tuberculosis) and take a hike outdoors at least once a week.

Most feature-length films were silent prior to 1930, after which sound film and the "talkies" signaled the Golden Age of Hollywood that would last through a decade of political and economic challenges. The tumultuous times catalyzed widespread popularity of risky and risqué behavior depicted in adventure and horror films, such as *Cleopatra* and *The Mummy*. There was particular concern over the effects of viewing films that were increasingly sexually explicit. Adults, including lawmakers, believed Hollywood movies were a major cause of teenage delinquency.[11]

Around 1930 religious and educational groups called for federal regulation of the movie industry. Rather than face government intervention, the heads of movie studios adopted a moral-focused code, called the Hays Code. By 1934 all movies were required to have certificates of approval by the Production Code Administration. But the code proved to be ineffective and highly restrictive. Morally questionable content frequently made it past the censors. The code lasted until 1968, when the Motion Picture Association of America began using a film rating system (G, M, R, and X) that lessened restrictions on filmmaking and placed moral responsibility on the film audience. Currently, rating codes are used to label films, TV programs, music, and video games to inform the public as to the specific nature of the media content with regards to violence, sexual content, and/or explicit language.

Taken together, film, TV, and radio were all considered powerful socialization agents for young people. In *Images of American Life: A History of Ideological Management in Schools* education scholar Joel Spring notes the dramatic, almost excessive, mediation of childhood:

> By the 1930s, youngsters might attend school during weekday hours, listen to the radio in the evening, and attend movies on the weekends. Whether sitting by the radio at home or in rows in schools or movie houses, children received a consciously constructed vision of the workings of the world.[12]

Questionable media content generated fear in adults and the need to protect children and adolescents from harmful media content. Various groups contended over film content, as movies during that time were considered a form of public education. Advocacy groups (including religious organizations) fought for censorship of sexual material in broadcast media and against sex education courses in public schools.

At the same time that parents and advocacy groups warned of the moral dangers of Hollywood films, they used film to weave an alternative narrative about public health and morality. While the United States was fighting a war against tuberculosis in the 1930s, the educational sector promoted health and hygiene as vehicles for social acceptance. In 1941 Cornell University produced a film, *For Health and Happiness*, that showed children of all ages in playful interactivity while a deep, matriarchal voiceover explained the importance of balanced nutrition and physical activity. In 1948 Cornell and McGraw-Hill produced *Body Care and Grooming*, to illustrate the value of good grooming and a "healthy" appearance among college students. The ten-minute film provided medical perspectives of skin, nail, and hair care, and a culturally gendered approach to dress and hygiene. A 1949 film by Coronet Instructional Films, *Exercise and Health*, depicts the result of sick, lonely, and tense teenagers engaging in regular athletics and team sports such as basketball, badminton, dance, and acrobatics. The film linked physical activity with increased personal confidence, social popularity, acceptance, and success.[13]

Mass media messages of the mid-twentieth century portrayed adolescence as a troubled period in the lives of young people, particularly among the populations of working class and poor. During just the first half of 1943, twelve hundred articles on the subject of juvenile delinquency appeared in popular magazines.[14] Adults continued to protect teenagers during 1940s wartime by establishing neighborhood teen recreation centers, also called "canteens." The Coca-Cola Company was an early corporate supporter of canteens where high school students could meet their friends and dance, which was the primary social activity among males and females.[15]

Following the end of WWII (between 1946 and 1951), more than twenty-two million children were born.[16] The baby boom coincided with an economic boom that allowed teenagers more freedom. Indulgence in food and media became the cultural soundtrack to adolescence throughout the 1940s. Teens consumed 190 million candy bars, 130 million soft drinks, 230 million sticks of gum, and 13 million ice cream bars per week.[17] Along with increased freedom came more adolescent spending power, especially on music.

Swing music was thought to be an "evil" contributor to juvenile delinquency, so state officials tried to outlaw jukeboxes.[18] Newspapers also drew links between rock 'n' roll and juvenile crime. Not surprisingly, radio stations banned songs with suggestive lyrics.[19] Despite the protests, the music industry made huge profits from affluent teenage audiences, especially white audiences drawn to the black musical styles of Elvis

Presley and Jerry Lee Lewis. When a Japanese company (currently known as Sony) released the first pocket size transistor radio in 1957, it was a "must-have" device among teenagers. No longer did families need to share one radio in the living room; teenagers could have their own device, their own music, and their own culture. Teenager became a brand unto itself.

Fast-forward to 2012 when 56 percent of American teens listened to music on broadcast radio (more than through iTunes downloads and/or CDs). Radio remains the primary source for teenagers to find out about new music. However, the most *popular* source for listening to music is YouTube, with 64 percent of teens listening and watching music through the online platform.[20] While current devices are highly if not primarily mobile, the added modality of viewing images while listening to music implies (although does not guarantee) a more evocative and potentially sedentary experience.

TV as (Processed) Food for Thought

The medium most blamed for the moral decline and increased sedentariness in America is the television. What we know today as TV was invented through the collective contributions of multiple inventors across multiple countries. In the United States, the advent of electronic television is attributed to a teenage farm boy named Philo Farnsworth who, in the 1920s, was encouraged by his high school science teacher to pursue his idea. Family legend is that Farnsworth would not allow his own children to watch TV, believing there was relatively little of importance that was on the air. Rather, it was the technology more so than medium (content) that was important to Farnsworth at this time.

Television brought together the multimedia dimensions of text, moving image, and sound. It signaled a shift back to the dominant use of the eye and the ear to combine images, text, and sound. In this sense, there was a return to orality—or what media ecologists call a "secondary orality." And this secondary orality was also highly constraining. TV was bound by space and time: a stationary box plugged into a fixed electrical outlet. The content was distributed according to a programmed schedule. In contrast, a book was much more flexible in terms of when and where the information could be consumed. The reader could go back and reread the previous page, whereas TV programming was in the moment and without memory. Like radio, and film, TV "spoke" to a mass audience, but provided little opportunity for audiences to speak back. The public health impact of TV was not as much in the programming itself. Rather, it was the ability to broadcast crucial information to the masses. At the same time, TV also detracted from physical activity and healthy eating.

TV was officially authorized as a commercial medium on July 1, 1941. The first TV commercial was a ten-second Bulova watch advertisement that ran before a baseball game. Watch Co., Sun Oil Co., Lever Bros. Co., and Procter & Gamble joined Bulova as the first sponsors of broadcast TV.[21] The 1940s food advertisements were primarily processed food inventions, included JELL-O instant pudding, EZ pop popcorn, PET evaporated milk, and Andersen canned split-pea soup.[22] TV marketing increased steadily through the 1950s with health product marketing through soap, vitamins, and toothpaste. Yet highly processed sugar-laden food products such as Bosco chocolate flavored syrup and Tootsie Pops permeated the airwaves.

Product endorsements by celebrities were prevalent as well. Instant Ovaltine was the official drink of the Secret Squadron, and viewers watched astronauts mix Tang Instant Beverage Drink. Clark Kent endorsed Kellogg's Sugar Smacks, Mike Wallace endorsed Golden Fluffo shortening, and Dennis James watched dancing packages of Old Gold cigarettes.

By 1969, tobacco companies were the single largest advertisers on TV. The proliferation of commercial TV synergized the growing concern over the effects of programming and advertising content. In response to pressure from public health advocates, on April 1, 1970, President Richard Nixon signed into legislation the Public Health Cigarette Smoking Act that officially banned cigarette ads on TV and radio and required the health warning on cigarette packages: "Warning: The Surgeon General Has Determined That Cigarette Smoking Is Dangerous to Your Health." However, marketing to children and teenagers increased and portrayed smoking as glamorous and desirable. Decades later, research revealed that more children ages five and six recognized Joe Camel than recognized Mickey Mouse or Fred Flintstone.[23] This signaled a heightened and longitudinal effort to protect children from harmful advertising.

The Impact of Instructional TV and Film

Researchers in the 1950s explored the subconscious of the human mind and warned the public of advertisers using exploitative strategies, such as motivational analysis, to manipulate young minds.[24] Strangely, educational researchers were unsuccessful in finding any significant influence of TV for classroom instruction. TV was perceived as an efficient new vehicle for public education, similar to books, radio, and film. In line with the emergent communication theories of the day, teaching and learning were thought of as the transmission and acquisition of information. Yet, educational research during the 1950s was unsuccessful in demonstrating any measurable advantages of televised over live instruction.[25] Similar to the early instructional films, instructional TV programs broadcasted the fundamentals of oral hygiene, where an instructor illustrated the correct method for brushing teeth.[26]

With the exception of specific propagandistic films, most of the early studies of instructional film evaluated the effects of film, rather than the characteristics of specific films.[27] In a comparison of two versions of a personal hygiene film, one a straight lecture (talking head) film and the other an embellished Hollywood version with music—both versions were found to be equally effective and were found to produce some type of change in personal hygiene behavior.[28] Hundreds of studies were conducted to determine the effectiveness of information transmission via TV as compared to other instructional formats. Without aid or follow-up from the teacher, instructional TV was found to be a largely ineffective teaching technology in the classroom.[29] This was quite a contrast from the controversy surrounding the effects of mass media upon adolescent youth.

The Perils of Advertising

In 1962 the Federal Communications Commission (FCC) concluded that children were neither qualified by age or experience to understand advertising messages. Yet, instead of government regulation, parents were called upon to regulate their children's viewing and media habits. In 1961 the U.S. Department of Health Education and Welfare published *Pogo Primer for Parents (TV Division)*. Authored by Walt Kelly, the twenty-four-page comic book "promoted healthy television viewing habits" based on "concepts of mental health and child rearing embodied in the findings of the 1960 White House Conference on Children and Youth." It suggests "T.V. watching could be a normal part of a balanced whole. Just like comic books, formal education and love . . . also milk."[30] The guide also stated: "It is not necessary to censor. It is necessary to guide,"[31] suggesting the progressive and pro-industrial mode of the times.

In the early 1970s the FCC assessed the fairness of targeting children with advertising. However, instead of banning advertising, they merely limited the amount of advertising time within children's programming and restricted advertising practices. With the growth of cable TV in the 1970s also came a dramatic increase in the amount of advertising to children through entire channels of programming and ads targeting a youth demographic.[32] Social science research of the 1960s and 1970s concluded that TV violence socialized young viewers into demonstrating aggressive behaviors and produced a narcotic-like effect among children. The TV industry resisted regulation and downplayed the impact of program content on children, particularly connections between violent programming and aggressive behavior.

Major criticisms of TV since its inception are its unrealistic portrayals of violence, drinking, smoking, and sex. In 1979 the surgeon general reported:

People must make personal lifestyle choices, too in the context of a society that glamorizes many hazardous behaviors through advertising and the mass media. Moreover, our society continues to support industries producing unhealthful products, enacts and enforces unevenly laws against behaviors such as driving while intoxicated, and offers ambiguous messages about the kinds of behavior that are advisable.[33]

In the 1980s, critics lamented TV as the "common school" that had replaced the traditional institutions of home, church, and public school as the primary agencies of education.[34] TV supplanted dinnertime conversation, and the TV set replaced the family room hearth.

Although commercial advertising was prevalent in schools and curriculum during the late 1970s, it heavily increased in the 1980s. Whittle Communications distributed to high schools a series of single-sponsored (commercial) wall posters, "Connections," and GO! magazine that targeted teenage girls through ads for a line of feminine hygiene products. Whittle also produced Special Reports distributed exclusively to doctors' waiting rooms, under the condition that no other magazine was available in the waiting room. Most notable is Whittle's Channel One programming, ten minutes of news programming and two minutes of commercial advertising, both targeted to teenagers. The high-energy program featured teen news correspondents reporting world events and special segments on issues of concern to adolescents. The two minutes of commercials advertised jeans, shoes, candy, and fast food.

With an initial investment of more than two hundred million dollars in the late 1980s, Channel One was the largest single introduction of television equipment to secondary schools in U.S. history. It also generated highly polemic responses across supporters and detractors alike. Supporters viewed the commercials as comparable to those that already pervaded homes as well as schools—in bulletin boards, cafeterias, magazines, newspapers, political posters, public service messaging, vending machines, and yearbooks. They considered it tolerable and even acceptable, not unlike McDonald's concessions in school cafeterias, soft drink vending machines in locker rooms, and Coca-Cola display ads on athletic scoreboards. One middle school principal stated: "Denying students access to technology to help them learn more is a greater ethical risk than controlled exposure to ads."[35]

Opponents maintain that the advertising violates the rights of students, relegating them to a captive audience since they are required by law to attend school. The proliferation of marketing messages in public schools also perpetuates the myth of health as a product (or series of products) for teens to avoid or acquire (depending upon the product) rather than health as a set of dispositional traits that govern behavior.

TV remains the primary advertising medium to reach children and adolescents. Young people ages twelve to fourteen see more food advertising than youth in any other age group, including fifteen- to seventeen-year-olds.[36] Teens between twelve and seventeen years of age view between fifteen and sixteen food ads per day, mostly for fast food, sugary cereals, restaurants, and candy—products that are high in saturated fat, sugar, or sodium.[37] In 2006, food marketers spent US$1 billion across all media (including TV and Internet) to market food (mostly unhealthy) to teens.[38] Companies spend more money on marketing sugary drinks to children and adolescents than on any other food category.[39] While the advertising expenditures and marketing strategies are pronounced, it is not clear the degree to which commercial advertising influences teen health behavior.

A HYPER-FOCUS ON MEDIA EFFECTS

The constancy among the rapid technological and social changes in the United States over the past two centuries is the excessive focus on the perceived and measured effects of media upon physical, mental, and emotional health. This is not a new concern, however. Roughly sixteen hundred years ago, Socrates warned that the written word would diminish the use of memory, and four hundred years ago, religious leaders denounced the printing press and the book as the greatest threats to civilization. Even a century ago, radio was thought to distract children from reading. And fifty years ago critics labeled TV as a threat to conversation, reading, and family life.[40]

When computers and the Internet emerged, similar criticisms were launched—that computers detract teens from forming real social relationships and the overload of information overwhelms their brains. Communication scholars Ellen Wartella and Nancy Jennings observe that with the advent of each new communications technology emerges the same responsive pattern: Proponents endorse the educational benefits while opponents express fear about exposure to inappropriate content.[41] They note that the cycle begins with concern over the level of access and the amount of time spent with the new medium, followed by concern about the media content and its effects on children. This pattern has repeated itself with radio, film, television, and now the Internet.

The medium that has been studied the most for its health effects on teenagers is television, as it is arguably the most ubiquitous modern communications medium and technology. Yet the actual effects of television upon health remain unclear. We know that TV viewing is *linked* with a cluster of unhealthy eating behaviors in adolescents, even after adjusting for socioeconomic and behavioral factors.[42] TV viewing is also *associated* with increased calorie intake, particularly of calorie-dense low-nutrient foods frequently advertised on television.[43] Longitudinal studies have consistently found that the more TV that adolescents watch, the more *likely* they are to gain excess weight.[44]

The act of TV viewing is even *associated with* reduced emotional health in adolescents.[45] Watching sexual content on TV is even found to *hasten* the initiation of sexual activity among teens.[46] The health literature indicates that alcohol advertising *increases the odds* of underage drinking, which is also *associated* with problematic behaviors, such as getting drunk, missing school, and getting into fights.[47] TV viewing is *linked to* spending less time doing homework.[48] Mass media are also found to *catalyze* eating disorders among females[49] through the promotion of thinness, dieting, and food deprivation, and as a source of information about eating disorders.[50]

Correlation is not causation, however, and one can also find research that consistently finds weak or little association between television viewing and obesity in children and adolescents.[51] In fact, a number of studies also show a weak or nonexistent relationship between physical activity and TV viewing.[52] Like the conundrum of obesity, the causes and effects of of TV viewing remain unclear.

Given the high frequency and duration of daily media use among teenagers and the volatility of adolescence, the concern over teenage vulnerability to message content is understandable. However, there is still much that is unknown about the singular influence of TV among teenagers. Still, federal policies focus on the harms of both media content and form in a visible effort to protect children, with less than successful results. For example, the 1996 Telecommunications Act called for the radio, TV, and film industries to develop voluntary ratings based on the degree of violent or sexual content. TV manufacturers were required by the year 2000 to install v-chips to enable parents to block programming.

The effectiveness of v-chips relies on the technological literacy and moral inclination of parents. The extent to which parents have control is debatable, as a child who reads the user manual will discover how to override the system by simply reseting the password. With the ubiquity of media content circulated across multiple platforms and environments, it is increasingly difficult if not impossible to shield children from sexual, violent, and even commercial content. Instead, we must equip teens with the moral judgment to govern themselves, wherever and whenever possible.

The bottom line is that both the medium and the message matter. Media guru Marshall McLuhan said it best: "The medium *is* the message." Yet protectionist efforts, such as banning junk food advertising or boycotting video games, may not be the best course in terms of increasing health among teens. Digital entrepreneur Clay Johnson warns against evading individual accountability by blaming the media:

> Blaming a medium or its creators for changing our minds and habits is like blaming food for making us fat. While it's certainly true that all new developments create the need for new warnings — until there was

fire, there wasn't a rule to not put your hand in it—conspiracy theories wrongly take free will and choice out of the equation.[53]

An agency approach to health literacy acknowledges the positive, negative, and unintended health effects of media use. For example, active video games that require players to physically move around may actually help to facilitate fitness and good health, although more research is needed to discover their potential. The ecology of media use also matters. Producers of children's media recognize this and tune into the interactions between player and platform. Again, more research is needed on the media ecology of young people, including the physiological, social, economic, and cultural factors that shape health behaviors.

WHAT MAKES A PUBLIC HEALTH MEDIA CAMPAIGN EFFECTIVE?

The advent of each new communications technology is accompanied by the assumption that dissemination of correct information will produce a change in public health attitudes, values, and behaviors—for better and also for worse. The traditional approach to health education is a top-down approach that assumes a direct causal relationship between health media and audiences. The assumption was that knowledge about diet, exercise, drugs, safety, oral health, sexuality, and relationships would develop certain attitudes that would lead to specific behavioral outcomes. The likelihood that public service advertising (PSA) campaigns will result in teens being less likely to use drugs, however, heavily depends upon how students make sense of the targeted media messages. Similar to the objectives of commercial media advertising, the objective of public health campaigns is to evoke cognitive and/or emotional responses that will lead to behavioral change. The success of mass media interventions and their effectiveness for public health is difficult to measure, however.

In 1981 after the drunk driving deaths of two hockey players at Wayland High School in Massachusetts, hockey coach Robert Anastas challenged students to be more proactive in doing something about the growing problem of drunk driving. He founded Students Against Driving Drunk (SADD) and along with a group of fifteen students, developed the Contract for Life, which he would later publish as a book. The SADD concept and chapters spread throughout the United States and is an example of successful school, community, and media advocacy. Although it is difficult to assess a change in teen behavior, the social change was significant: All fifty states passed a minimum drinking age law, and drunk driving fatalities decreased. In 1997, SADD adopted the new name of Students Against Destructive Decisions to encompass the growing number of social pressures facing teens (e.g., alcohol and drug use, suicide, violence, distracted driving). It is a successful example of youth leadership and governance.

In 1990 Congress passed the Children's Television Act (CTA), giving the FCC power to require TV stations to devote time to educational and informative programming. News broadcasts expanded their inclusion of health segments. News media coverage of specific cases of HIV/AIDS between 1985 and 1993 led to increased public awareness, knowledge, and public policy responses.[54] In 1997 the Centers for Disease Control and Prevention (CDC) collaborated with the entertainment industry on ways to reach the public with more accurate information about HIV.

The CDC also provided information and expert consultants to writers in Hollywood. Between 2009 and 2012, the program worked, with ninety-one TV series on thirty-one networks, and covered almost seven hundred topics in inquiries and briefings. The project also provided more than two thousand links to public health information on TV show websites.[55] Viewers of soap operas, prime-time TV shows, and talk shows reported learning something about a disease or how to prevent it and took action as a result.[56]

According to public health researchers, effective public health campaigns focus on well-designed messages that are "delivered to their intended audience with sufficient reach and frequency to be seen or heard and remembered."[57] By far the most prevalent research on mass media effects is in the area of tobacco use prevention. Since the 1990s, mass media campaigns have been associated with a decline in young people starting to smoke.[58] Over the past several decades, mass media campaigns have been used to change behaviors, such as preventing alcohol, tobacco, and illicit drug use, as well as heart disease prevention.[59] Research on the attitudes, beliefs, and behaviors of middle and high school students regarding substance use were significantly related to their exposure to antidrug television advertising.

Arguably the most successful public health media campaign is the "truth" campaign (www.thetruth.com) by the National Public Education Fund and directed by the American Legacy Foundation in 1999 as part of the Master Settlement Agreement between states and the tobacco industry. The campaign targets teens ages twelve to seventeen years of age with ads featuring "trendy youth involved in public demonstrations against the tobacco industry" to encourage youth "to rebel against the tobacco industry instead of rebelling with tobacco."[60] The approach is to "pull back the curtain" on the practices of the tobacco industry to reveal manipulative marketing practices.[61] The campaign was responsible for 22 percent of the observed decline in youth smoking between 1999 and 2002.[62]

Like media effects research, much of the research in public health education is grounded in the experimental hypothesis testing used in the natural sciences. A meta-analysis of research in the area of health-promoting media literacy indicates positive behavior-related outcomes as a result of media interventions.[63] Based on the perceived effects of media on health, U.S. agencies frame media literacy as a preventative measure or tool for reducing its negative effects. The U.S. Department of Health and Human Services and the White House National Drug Control Policy have identified media literacy as a preventative measure for drug abuse. The American Academy of Pediatrics also advocates media literacy as a preventative measure for the negative effects of tobacco, alcohol, and food marketing.

We must look at the constellation of factors in determining the success of a public health media campaign. Scientific methodology does not fully explain human behavior as humans are moral agents. Audience behavior is complex and grounded in, among other things, cognition, skills, motivation, intentions, and demographic factors. More research is needed to understand the intersection of media and interpersonal communication and the general media ecology of adolescent health. From this perspective, public health advertising that focuses on the individual at the ignorance of systemic forces may prove ineffective.[64]

Public health campaigns often compete with social norms and contradicting messages within the wider media environment.[65] Given the history of industrialization and commerce in the United States, it is therefore not surprising that public health media campaigns that are pro-consumption (i.e., eat more fruits, drink nonfat milk) are more effective than those that focused on reducing consumption (i.e., fat intake, sugar).[66] The public health media campaigns that are more likely to be successful are those that also have *multiple interventions and are episodic* (i.e., health screenings and vaccinations) rather than habitual (i.e., food choices, sun exposure, physical activity). The success of such campaigns in effecting healthy behavior also hinges on direct public access to the required resources, such as healthy foods.[67]

Campaigns targeted at parents of youth have more success in drug use prevention than those targeted toward youth directly.[68] Behavioral change is also more likely when media efforts are combined with school and community programs.[69] A meta-analysis of studies on the effects of media campaigns found that campaigns that supplemented their media messages with other components had stronger effects than those with just the singular media message.[70] For example, seat belt, oral health, and alcohol campaigns have traditionally been successful, with the most success found in campaigns that have a law enforcement component.[71] Similarly, public health campaigns combined with other strategies (like school programs) are effective in changing behavior.[72,73]

The anti-smoking campaigns succeeded on a national scale to reduce smoking across income and educational levels and across race and gender. The campaign included educational programs, public service announcements, and laws that banned smoking in public places. As a collective, these measures made a deep impact on reducing smoking.

NEW TECHNOLOGIES, NEW CHALLENGES

Throughout history, media technologies have served as powerful communication channels to persuade the public in ways that can improve health and also to thwart it. Undoubtedly, the print and electronic epochs afforded an unprecedented level of information distribution to the masses. This enabled the public to take advantage of scientific discoveries in real time. The use of media also transformed how scientists see and interact with the natural world. On the other hand, there is an overabundance of information in an increasingly technologized world. For teenagers, navigating daily life is a series of mediated experiences where someone in authority attempts to shape their attitudes, beliefs, and behaviors—often without their knowledge or consent.

The unanticipated consequences of technological evolution present both opportunities and challenges to the growth and development of teenagers. From anti-smoking to anti-soda, anti-alcohol, and other counter-message public media health campaigns, the communication approach is essentially the same: to influence behavior. In this sense, public health campaigns employ the same rhetorical devices used by advertisers, marketing professionals, and public relations specialists. Ultimately, those who have access to and control of the information environment will determine the purpose and quite possibly the outcome of health messaging.

Conceptualizing public health as primarily the search for remedies or cures for ailments is a similar problem to defining media literacy as the search for audience protection from the perceived harmful effects of media. Through and across the broadcasting era of the twentieth century the focus has been the protection of young people from the harms of media content and form(s). This inoculation approach has largely been ineffective in that it assumes all audiences interpret media messages in essentially the same way. A more progressive approach is proactive rather than protectionist and empowers teenagers within a media environment that is continuously evolving and increasingly complex. The next chapter explores the digital landscape and suggests critical questions to guide teens on their journey.

NOTES

1. George Miller Beard, *Neurasthenia as a Cause of Inebriety*. Hartford, CT: Hartford Press, 1879.

2. Robert S. Lynd and Helen Merrell Lynd, *Middletown: A Study in Modern American Culture*. New York: Harcourt Brace & Company, 1929, 255.

3. Paula S. Fass, *The Damned and the Beautiful: American Youth in the 1920s*. London: Oxford University Press, 1979.

4. John Modell and Madeline Goodman, "Historical Perspectives," in *At the Threshold: The Developing Adolescent*, ed. S. Shirley Feldman and Glen. R. Elliots. Cambridge, MA: Harvard University Press, 1990.

5. Grace Palladino, *Teenagers: An American History*. New York: Basic Books, 1996, 53.

6. Sarah Mondale and Sarah B. Patton, eds., *School: The Story of American Public Education*. Boston: Beacon Press, 2001, 113.

7. Christopher H. Sterling and John Michael Kittross, *Stay Tuned: A History of American Broadcasting*, 3rd ed. Mahwah, NJ: Lawrence Erlbaum Associates, 2001.

8. J. Michael Sproule, "Social Responses to Twentieth-Century Propaganda," in *Propaganda: A Pluralistic Perspective*, ed. T. J. Smith III, 5–22. New York: Praeger, 1989.

9. Renee Hobbs and Amy Jensen, "The Past, Present, and Future of Media Literacy Education," *Journal of Media Literacy Education* 1, no. 1 (2009): 1–11.

10. Kathryn H. Fuller, *At the Picture Show: Small-Town Audiences and the Creation of Movie Fan Culture*. Charlottesville: University of Virginia Press, 2001.

11. Lynd and Lynd, *Middletown*, 267–68.

12. Joel Spring, *Images of American Life: A History of Ideological Management in Schools, Movies, Radio and Television*. New York: SUNY Press, 1992, 13.

13. Each of these videos are available for viewing at the Internet Archive located at http://www.archive.org.

14. Palladino, *Teenagers*, 82.

15. Palladino, *Teenagers*, 86.

16. Susan J. Douglas, *Where the Girls Are: Growing Up Female with the Mass Media*. New York: Random House, 1995, 22.

17. Palladino, *Teenagers*, 110.

18. Palladino, *Teenagers*, 83.

19. Palladino, *Teenagers*, 127.

20. Marketing Charts, "Radio Still Primary Source of New Music; Popular with Teens," August 17, 2012, http://www.marketingcharts.com/radio/radio-still-americans-primary-source-of-new-music-popular-with-teens-22997/.

21. Jeff Miller, "A U.S. Television Chronology, 1875–1970," http://jeff560.tripod.com/chronotv.html.

22. "Class Commercials, 1940s–1960s," July 20, 2010, http://www.youtube.com/watch?v=iaTZY7be2EY.

23. Paul M. Fischer, Meyer P. Schwartz, John W. Richards Jr, Adam O. Goldstein, and Tina H. Rojas, "Brand Logo Recognition by Children Aged 3 to 6 Years. Mickey Mouse and Old Joe the Camel," *Journal of the American Medical Association* 266, no. 22 (December 11, 1991): 3145–48.

24. Vance Packard, *The Hidden Persuaders*. New York: David McKay & Company, 2007.

25. Lionel C. Barrow and Bruce H. Westley, "Comparative Teaching Effectiveness of Radio and Television," *AV Communication Review* 7, no. 1 (1959): 14–23.

26. Edwin B. Kurtz, *Pioneering in Educational Television, 1932–1939: A Documentary Presentation*. Des Moines: State University of Iowa Press, 1959.

27. Joseph J. Weber, "Comparative Effectiveness of Some Visual Aids in Seventh Grade Instruction," *Educational Screen*. Entire issue. 1922. See also J. J. Stein, "The Effect of a Pre-Film Test on Learning from an Educational Sound Motion Picture." Tech Report No. SDC 269-7-35. Port Washington, NY: United States Naval Training Device Center, Office of Naval Research, 1952; A. A. Lumsdaine, R. L. Sulzer, and F. F. Kopstein, "The Effect of Animation Cues and Repetition of Examples on Learning from an Instructional Film." HRRL Report No. 24. Washington, DC: United States Air Force Human Factors Research Lab, 1961.

28. A. W. VanderMeer. "Relative Effectiveness of Color and Black and White in Instructional Films." Tech Rep. No. SDC 269-7-28. Port Washington, NY: United States Naval Training Device Center, Office of Naval Research, 1952.

29. Paul Saettler, *A History of Instructional Technology*. New York: McGraw-Hill, 1968. See also Wilbur Schramm, ed., *Educational Television: The Next Ten Years*. Stanford, CA: Institute for Communication Research, 1962.

30. Walt Kelly, *Pogo Primer for Parents*. Washington, DC: U.S. Department of Health, Education and Welfare, 1961, 23.

31. Kelly, *Pogo Primer for Parents*, 26.

32. Brian L. Wilcox, Dale Kunkel, Joanne Cantor, Peter Dowrick, Susan Linn, and Edward Palmer, "Report of the APA Task Force on Advertising and Children." Washington, DC: American Psychological Association, February 20, 2004.

33. U.S. Department of Health, Education and Welfare, *Healthy People: The Surgeon General's Report on Health Promotion and Disease Prevention*. Washington, DC: U.S. Government Printing Office, 1979.

34. Neil Postman, *Amusing Ourselves to Death: Public Discourse in the Age of Show Business*. New York: Penguin Books, 1985.

35. M. Kollasch, "Switching Channels: Using TV to Teach about TV," *Wilson Library Bulletin* 65, no. 1 (1990): 66.

36. Cathryn R. Dembek, Jennifer L. Harris, and Marlene B. Schwartz, *Where Children and Adolescents View Food and Beverage Ads on TV: Exposure by Channel and Program*. New Haven, CT: Rudd Center for Food Policy & Obesity, Yale University, March 2013, 18, http://www.yaleruddcenter.org/resources/upload/docs/what/reports/Rudd_Report_TV_Ad_Exposure_Channel_Program_2013.pdf.

37. Dembek, Harris, and Schwartz, *Where Children and Adolescents View Food and Beverage Ads on TV*.

38. *Marketing Food to Children and Adolescents: A Review of Industry Expenditure, Activities, and Self-Regulation*. Washington, DC: Federal Trade Commission, 2008.

39. *Marketing Food to Children and Adolescents*.

40. Vaughan Bell, "Don't Touch That Dial! A History of Media Technology Scares, from the Printing Press to Facebook," *Slate*, February 15, 2010, http://www.slate.com/articles/health_and_science/science/2010/02/dont_touch_that_dial.html.

41. Ellen A. Wartella and Nancy Jennings, "Children and Computers: New Technology — Old Concerns," *Future of Children* 10, no. 2 (2000): 31–43.

42. Leah M. Lipsky and Ronald J. Iannotti, "Associations of Television Viewing with Eating Behaviors in the 2009 Health Behaviour in School-Aged Children Study," *Archives of Pediatrics and Adolescent Medicine* 166, no. 5 (2012): 465–72, doi: 10.1001/archpediatrics.2011.1407.

43. Jean L. Wiecha, Karen E. Peterson, David S. Ludwig, Juhee Kim, Arthur Sobol, and Steven L. Gortmaker, "When Children Eat What They Watch: Impact of Television Viewing on Dietary Intake in Youth," *Archives of Pediatric and Adolescent Medicine* 160, no. 4 (2006): 436–42, doi: 10.1001/archpedi.160.4.436.

44. Juan P. Rey-López, Germán Vicente-Rodriguez, Mercedes Biosca, and Luis A. Moreno, "Sedentary Behaviour and Obesity Development in Children and Adolescents," *Nutrition, Metabolism and Cardiovascular Diseases* 18 (2008): 242–51.

45. Kristen Harrison, "Scope of Self: Toward a Model of Television's Effects on Self-Complexity in Adolescence," *Communication Theory* 16 (2006): 251–79.

46. Rebecca L. Collins, Marc N. Elliott, Sandra H. Berry, David E. Kanouse, Dale Kunkel, Sarah B. Hunter, and Angela Miu, "Watching Sex on Television Predicts Adolescent Initiation of Sexual Behavior," *Pediatrics* 114, no. 3 (September 2004), e280–e289.

47. Jerry L. Grenard, Clyde W. Dent, and Alan W. Stacy, "Exposure to Alcohol Advertisements and Teenage Alcohol-Related Problems," *Pediatrics* 131, no. 2 (January 28, 2013), doi: 10.1542/peds.2012-1480.

Chapter 2

48. Elizabeth A. Vandewater, David S. Bickham, and June H. Lee, "Time Well Spent? Relating Television Use to Children's Free-Time Activities," *Pediatrics* 117, no. 2 (2006): e181–e191.

49. Wendy Spettigue and Katherine A. Henderson, "Eating Disorders and the Role of the Media," *The Canadian Child and Adolescent Psychiatry Review* 13, no. 1 (2004): 16–19.

50. Anne M. Morris and Debra K. Katzman, "The Impact of the Media on Eating Disorders in Children and Adolescents," *Paediatrics and Child Health* 8, no. 5 (2003): 287–89.

51. Thomas N. Robinson and Joel D. Killen, "Ethnic and Gender Differences in the Relationships between Television Viewing and Obesity, Physical Activity, and Dietary Fat Intake," *Journal of Health Education* 26 (1995): S91–S98.

52. Robinson and Killen, "Ethnic and Gender Differences." See also Thomas N. Robinson, Lawrence D. Hammer, Joel D. Killen, Helena C. Kramer, Darrell. M. Wilson, Chris Hayward, and C. Barr Taylor, "Does Television Viewing Increase Obesity and Reduce Physical Activity? Cross-Sectional and Longitudinal Analyses among Adolescent Girls," *Pediatrics* 91 (1993): 273–80; Robert H. DuRant, Tom Baranowski, Maribeth Johnson, and William O. Thompson, "The Relationship among Television Watching, Physical Activity, and Body Composition of Young Children," *Pediatrics* 94 (1994): 449–55.

53. Clay Johnson, *The Information Diet: A Case for Conscious Consumption*. Sebastopol, CA: O'Reilly Media, 2012, 24.

54. National Research Council, *The Future of the Public's Health in the 21st Century*. Washington, DC: National Academies Press, 2003, 310.

55. Hollywood, Health & Society, History/Stats, http://hollywoodhealthandsociety. org/about-us/history-stats.

56. Centers for Disease Control, "1999 Healthstyles Survey: Soap Opera Viewers and Health Information," 2002, http://www.cdc.gov/healthcommunication/ toolstemplates/entertainmented/1999survey.html.

57. Lorien C. Abroms and Edward W. Maibach, "The Effectiveness of Mass Communication to Change Public Behavior," *Annual Review of Public Health* 29 (2008): 221, doi: 10.1146/annurev.publhealth.29.020907.090824. See also J. T. Bertrand, K. O'Reilly, J. Denison, R. Anhang, and M. Sweat, "Systematic Review of the Effectiveness of Mass Communication Programs to change HIV/AIDS-related Behaviors in Developing Countries," *Health Educ. Res.* 21, no. 4 (2006): 586.

58. National Cancer Institute, "The Role of the Media in Promoting and Reducing Tobacco Use," Tobacco Control Monograph No 19. NIH Pub No 07-6242. Bethesda, MD: U.S. Department of Health and Human Services, National Institutes of Health, National Cancer Institute, 2008.

59. Melanie A. Wakefield, Barbara Loken, and Robert C Hornik, "Use of Mass Media Campaigns to Change Health Behavior," *Lancet* 376 (2010): 1268, doi: 10.1016/ S01406736(10)60809-4.

60. Jeffrey J. Hicks, "The Strategy behind Florida's 'Truth' Campaign," *Tobacco Control* 10 (2001): 1–2.

61. "Pulling Back the Curtain," http://www.thetruth.com/about/.

62. Abroms and Maibach, "The Effectiveness of Mass Communication," 222.

63. Se-Hoon Jeong, Hyunyi Cho, and Yoori Hwang, "Media Literacy Interventions: A Meta-Analytic Review," *Journal of Communication* 62 (2012): 454–72.

64. Lori Dorfman and Lawrence Wallack, "Advertising Health: The Case for Counter-Ads," *Public Health Reports* 108, no. 6 (1993): 716–26.

65. Wakefield, Loken, and Hornik, "Use of Mass Media," 1268.

66. Wakefield, Loken, and Hornik, "Use of Mass Media," 1265.

67. Wakefield, Loken, and Hornik, "Use of Mass Media."

68. James H. Derzon and Mark W. Lipsey. "A Meta-Analysis of the Effectiveness of Mass-Communication for Changing Substance-Use Knowledge, Attitudes, and Behav-

ior," in *Mass Media and Drug Prevention: Classic and Contemporary Theories and Research,* ed. W. D. Crano and M. Burgoon, 231–58. Mahwah, NJ: Erlbaum, 2002.

69. National Cancer Institute, "The Role of the Media."

70. Derzon and Lipsey, "A Meta-Analysis of the Effectiveness of Mass-Communication."

71. Leslie B. Snyder and Mark A. Hamilton, "A Meta-Analysis of U.S. Health Campaign Effects on Behavior: Emphasize, Enforcement, Exposure, and New Information, and Beware the Secular Trend," in *Public Health Communication: Evidence for Behavior Change,* ed. R. C. Hornik, 357–84. Mahwah, NJ: Lawrence Erlbaum, 2002.

72. Brian S. Flynn, John K. Worden, Roger H. Secker-Walker, Gary J. Badger, Berta M. Geller, and Michael C. Costanza, "Prevention of Cigarette Smoking through Mass Media Intervention and School Programs," *American Journal of Public Health* 82 (1992): 827–34.

73. Brian S. Flynn, John K. Worden, Roger H. Secker-Walker, Phyllis L. Pirie, Gary J. Badger, Joseph H. Carpenter, and Berta M. Geller, "Mass Media and School Interventions for Cigarette Smoking Prevention: Effects 2 Years after Completion," *American Journal of Public Health* 84, no. 7 (1994): 1148–50.

THREE

Teen Health: Is There an App for That?

The advent and growth of the World Wide Web in the early 1990s was a boon to scientists and researchers who wanted to rapidly share and decentralize information. In the field of public health, the Internet afforded mass distribution of essential information to diverse audiences and public access to health experts—without the expense and gatekeeping associated with traditional media. During the twentieth century, voices in radio, TV, and film were far less in number and diversity than the voices in print.

However, the Information Age granted Internet users a vast World Wide Web of health information and access to a global audience. In the twenty-first century, social and global networks radically disrupted traditional ways of broadcasting information about health and ways of influencing health behaviors. Public health communication has morphed into an era of transmedia—where oral, print, broadcast, and digital media converge. This requires more advanced cognitive skills as well as social skills. This chapter delves into the ways in which adolescent youth transnavigate this physical as well as digital terrain, and outlines key questions to guide them on this journey.

HEALTH COMMUNICATION 2.0

Digital media occupy a significant amount of teenagers' time, energy, learning, and social development outside of formalized schooling. Teens spend approximately 7.5 hours a day using various media technologies.[1] Instant messaging (IM), text messaging, and blogging are the most popular uses of the Internet and computers among teens.[2] Teens are technically skilled at editing, remixing, and (re)creating their social identities.[3] Online social networks (such as Facebook, Tumblr, Pinterest, and Twitter) allow users to create profiles, message, and share multimedia content with a global audience. Roughly 75 percent of online teens have created online content and 21 percent have remixed online content.[4] Unlike young children, teens are more likely to be media multitaskers.[5] They use the Internet in ways that are both social and commercial.[6] Research reports 66 percent of teens online use the Internet to research a purchase or new product and 31 percent use the Internet to buy a product.[7, 8]

When it comes to the health and safety of children and teens using the Internet, the protection of privacy has long been a concern of the federal government. The 2000 Children's Online Privacy Protection Act (COPPA) restricts commercial websites from collecting personal information from children under age thirteen. Numerous companies violate this law, however.

Most recently the Federal Trade Commission (FTC) has penalized Girls Life, Inc.,[9] Mrs. Fields Cookies, and Hershey Foods.[10] Even within the bounds of the law, it is difficult for children and teens to discern trustworthy health information from advertising and other public relations mechanisms. "Cookies" stored on a user's computer track online activity and report user data back to the marketer. Additionally, online "reward programs" (such as those of soda and junk food marketers) and advertising through social media (e.g., Facebook, Twitter, smart phone apps) attract teenagers. For example, My Coke Rewards allows consumers to accumulate points for purchases and then redeem them for prizes. The program collects large amounts of personal data from participants, allowing Coke to refine its marketing efforts. The consumer, on the other hand, must purchase hundreds of bottles of Coca-Cola product to reap any tangible rewards.

One model that provides easy access to high-quality health information is Go Ask Alice! originally launched by Columbia University in 1993 as a health question and answer intranet website for its college students and then in 1994 for the entire Web. Its mission was to provide readers with "reliable, accurate, accessible, culturally competent information and a range of thoughtful perspectives so that they can make responsible decisions concerning their health and well-being."[11] In 1994 Columbia University took Go Ask Alice! live on the Web to the general public. In 2002, Go Ask Alice! partnered with MTV for the "Fight for Your Rights" sexual health campaign, and over the decades has won numerous awards. Go Ask Alice! remains an active public health education website with 1.7 million visitors each month.[12] Health communication scholars identify Go Ask Alice! as a successful example of a commercial-free web-based expert system that can have "impressive effects on individual health beliefs, attitudes, and behavior."[13, 14]

While teens may use social media technology in ways that transcend the medium, at the same time they are still developing an understanding of abstract concepts, ideologies, values, and how to develop an awareness of a larger community and common good. There is much they do not yet understand about larger institutional forces that shape their understanding and enactment of online behaviors.

Bridging the Digital Health Divide

Until fairly recently there existed a digital divide between those who had access to the Internet and those who did not. The proliferation of the Internet in schools and libraries in recent decades has enabled sharing of information like never before. One localized example is the AllerSchool system that debuted in a Colorado Springs school district in 2011. Aller School enables parents of children with severe food allergies to register their child with the district's Food and Nutrition Services. Parents can log into the district's weekly menu website to see the exact ingredients of each food item that will be served on each school day. Providing parents with a breakdown of menu ingredients in turn affords critical reflection and subsequent modification of menus by the districts' food service staff. The web-based software program provides parents access to crucial information. Yet continued lack of public access combined with a paucity of technical skills continue to prevent the most vulnerable and needy populations from accessing crucial health information.

On a national level, the United States Department of Agriculture (USDA) offers SuperTracker, a free, healthy eating planning and tracking tool at ChooseMyPlate.gov. Its purpose is to help individuals plan, analyze, and track diet and physical activity and customize their health goal. Fooducate is another website and software application that allows a shopper to use a smartphone camera to scan the barcode of a product and get a rating of its nutritional value, based on ingredients and a database of foods. The app gives the food a letter grade and, if available, supplies healthier alternatives. The Center for Science in the Public Interest (CSPI) also offers a Chemical Cuisine glossary on the various additives to processed foods and how harmful they may be. It is available as a smartphone app to use while shopping. These types of apps provide the consumer with information on demand. The catch is that consumers must perceive it as a felt need and then intentionally seek out the information.

The World Wide Web is essentially a vast wilderness where prestigious research institutions coexist with highly commercial entities, among other entities. Despite providing essentially free access to vast amounts of data, the Internet poses a major challenge to the quality and reliability of health information. This requires critical literacy skills that extend well beyond mere access to information. Erica Austin and Bruce Pinkelton at the University of Washington concluded that ease of access to high-quality information is only the first step; media literacy skills to navigate and critically evaluate pertinent, accurate, and credible information are essential.[15] Austin and Pinkelton studied college students during an outbreak of the H1N1 flu virus and found that students who self-diagnosed correctly showed higher-level skills in their ability to acquire information, analyze and compare information from multiple sources, and correctly evaluate sources for their expertise. In contrast, college students who self-diagnosed incorrectly relied upon information being easily accessible.

From an interdisciplinary perspective, librarians and media specialists are highly valuable in their ability to facilitate information literacy—to empower teachers and students to locate and make sense of credible health-related information.[16] Accessing and assessing health-related information is not enough, however. It must lead to action. Media literacy educator Renee Hobbs also cautions against relying too heavily on direct access to information as the sole solution to a community's information needs. In *Digital and Media Literacy: A Plan of Action* she writes:

> Emerging technologies may help people sift, organize and evaluate information. But even tech-savvy individuals are unlikely to possess the institutional resources they need to meet all their personal information needs and objectives without help. No individual can generate all the analysis, debate, context and interpretation necessary to turn raw information into useful knowledge.[17]

Ultimately, it comes down to more than access to technology or even technological proficiency. Health literacy hinges on the ability of teens to think critically about media *and to enact* positive media and health-related behaviors in ways that are both conscientious and competent. This requires not just digital connectivity to information, but social connectivity as well.

Crowdsourcing Health

At both macro- and microlevels, the use of current media technologies to individually and collectively support positive health behaviors is groundbreaking. Mobile devices, including cell phones, and social media not only provide a public gateway for health information; they also serve as a vehicle for health research by supplying portals for crowdsourced data that are fed back to the public.

On a macrolevel, the use of mapping software can visually illustrate food store locations, sales density, health statistics, and demographic data to show the relationship between income, supermarket sales, and diet-related deaths. Such technological tools are powerful for identifying and addressing health inequities that exist on local, national, and even global levels. Public health officials also use Facebook and Twitter for data gathering during an emergency. They can also text message information about new cases of influenza from hospital settings and do risk-mapping through the use of global positioning systems.

Public health researchers have found that social network analyses can predict flu outbreaks earlier than traditional tracking methods.[18] The website Flu Near You allows individuals to serve as "potential disease sentinels" by reporting their health status on a weekly basis.[19] The smartphone application Outbreaks Near Me delivers a global map of outbreaks of various illnesses reported around the world. This birdseye view can greatly assist in the prevention and containment of outbreaks. The uses of social media by public health agencies is still in its infancy and are used primarily to broadcast information, rather than to engage, interact, or create conversation. News reporting of the 2014 Ebola epidemic has taught us that too much information can stir up fear in ways that are detrimental to the rights of individuals.

On a microlevel, individuals can use technology to make objective assessments of their health in ways never before possible. Individuals can assess physical activity through the use of portable accelerometers—including sensors, microcomputer processors, memory storage, and wireless communication. The individual use of smartphones, wireless wrist monitors, and other mobile devices enables individuals to communicate directly with doctors and make healthcare decisions based on a collaborative approach to data collection and analysis. Doctors are also experimenting with anonymous social support networks (similar to those of Alcoholics Anonymous) to help obese teens cope with their condition. The website Weigh2Rock.com is one example where adolescent users are paired with a weight loss partner for moral support, motivation, and problem solving.

The Hazards of Data Personalization

On one hand, the personalization of data elegantly aligns with constructivist approaches to learning. Software programs like Fitnessgram allow teens to set and track their individual fitness goals. The idea behind the technology is to "minimize comparisons between children and emphasize personal fitness for health rather than goals based solely on performance."[20] There also exist many other mobile device applications that assess dietary intake and send motivational text messages to increase fruit and vegetable consumption while decreasing junk food consumption. The increase in mindfulness about health behaviors is generally a beneficial one, and there are a plethora of technological tools to support these uses.

However, left unchecked, our self-directed uses of technology have become so excessive in their user-centeredness that it results in more data than we know how to handle. Cultural critic Alyssa Quart notes that Americans have become self-quantifiers or "scientists of our own lives," in our obsession with self-tracking and measuring our diet, exercise, sleep habits, body mass index (BMI), marital relationships, commuter travel, and even brain functions.[21] While such self-quantification may bring empowerment and self-reliance on one hand, therein also lies the danger of assuming that more data collection automatically leads to self-improvement. The downside is that too much data can also be distracting and self-destructive.

The "Healthy School Meals Realized through Technology (SMART) Schools" debuted in April 2014 as a collaborative effort of Rush Canyon Ranch Institute, the UNO Charter School Network, the City of Chicago, A+ Café (a school nutrition software company), and the Hillshire Brands Company.[22] The pilot project uses technology in school cafeterias to track what each sixth-grade student eats. Cafeteria workers scan each student's identification card and use a touch-screen monitor to record each food item the student chooses for breakfast and lunch. The system allows researchers to document students' food choices and create a summary of their nutritional value.

Each week, parents and teachers receive a comprehensive report on the nutritional value of their child's school meals along with healthy eating recommendations for each student. While this project presents opportunities for parental engagement and parent education around issues of childhood obesity, it also raises questions as to how the data are used for health literacy education among the sixth-grade students. To what extent are they learning to make healthy choices on their own? And how, if at all, are student data used beyond the cafeteria for noneducational purposes?

What happens when the data or technology itself (rather than teen health) becomes the object of focus, as with eating disorders such as anorexia? Too much focus on the technology itself puts the onus on the individual and detracts from systemic factors that may be inhibiting, rather than promoting, optimal health. The obsession extends further than self-measurement as we then share these data with friends on Facebook, Twitter, or even just to store "in the cloud," where it no longer becomes our personal property and can even be exploited by those who profit from data.

The personalization and mobility afforded by new communications technologies appear to empower us individually, yet corporations use our personal data in ways that benefit the marketplace. This threatens not only our individual privacy, but also the strength of communities and entire populations. In a postdigital age, it is increasingly difficult to ensure that personal (health) information can be manageable (not overwhelming), confidential, secure, and private. It is a serious matter that the health of our teenagers is no longer a private issue but a public commodity.

T2X: A TRANSMEDIA APPROACH TO TEEN HEALTH

The crowdsourcing of adolescent health through transmediated experiences is exemplified by the 2009 collaborative T2x (www.T2x.me) project involving the National Institute of Health; University of California, Los Angeles; Health Net, Inc.; and EPG Technologies. T2x was conceptualized as a teens-only health literacy online social network designed to address the challenges faced by 93 percent of California teens (ages thirteen to eighteen) who have access to health insurance but are not skilled in navigating the healthcare system.[23] The goal of T2x was to see if an online social network would increase low-income teens' capacity to access and use their health insurance, become more engaged in their healthcare decisions, and develop pro-health attitudes. In January 2012 the program was expanded nationwide.

T2x houses more than sixteen hundred health articles written specifically for teens on topics such as nutrition, fitness, stress management, substance abuse, and anti-bullying. Beyond access to health information, the online community houses competitions, games, quizzes, blogs, video sharing, and other transmedia tools. Teens can share their health concerns and chat online with health experts and with each other (Health Net members can directly access the nurse advice line as part of their healthcare benefits). Areas of health "expertise" include sex, sexually transmited diseases, relationships, infectious diseases, and addiction. All chats are managed and conversations logged. The level of information is customized to the teen user; by texting keywords to a designated number the user can receive important health-related texts on their mobile device.

Empowerment, self-expression, and responsibility are key values associated with T2x. Teens can upload video content and photos. Users can see activities and upcoming events in their local community. They can set new goals or use one that another user has created, such as "Lose Weight." The social support and associated materials for that goal are stored for each individual user. Users can also create and contribute to discussions on a range of topics (from music to health) on bulletin boards. In addition, users can link their T2x account with Facebook and Twitter. Beyond social networking, T2x is a powerful example of leveraging transmedia storytelling—telling different parts of the story using different media forms—to more effectively engage teens to facilitate their transition into adulthood. Because the user experience is highly participatory, it allows the teenager to shape his or her own learning experience and on their own terms.

The most educationally innovative aspect of T2x is the ability to create microsites or "Spaces" within T2x that afford a customizable experience. The "Club" project is a story that unfolds in a series of webisodes about a group of students who are members of their school's Health Club. Real students from a local performing arts school star in the short videos. The first webisode debuted in May 2011 and introduces the characters, beginning with Lucas who, after being caught smoking on school grounds, is punished by the principal requiring him to join the school's Health Club alongside a group of "nerdy health-obsessed misfits."[24] "Club" users can participate in discussions with cast members, and additional content is added to the site in "real time" as users interact with the characters to create their own experience. T2x also provides a mixture of mobile and online (and classroom-based) activities. Teachers can use this as part of classroom curriculum and extend the learning beyond the classroom with short message service (SMS) technology on mobile devices. Self-contained topic-oriented stories are also available on the site for classes who visit the site during sustained blocks of time.

The main purpose of T2x was to increase low-income teens' capacity to access and use their health insurance and to be "knowledgeable health care consumers."[25] Yet T2x is significant in ways beyond its original goal, as seen in initial research findings. The "ReThink Your Drink" Campaign fostered critical thinking among adolescents about consuming high-caloric beverages. Research about T2x found a 71 percent improvement in health knowledge, 54 percent improvement in attitude, and 75 percent improvement in "intent for behavior change."

The educational potential for T2x lies in its creative uses of transmedia storytelling to improve health literacy among teenagers. Still, the highly personalized nature of T2x raises important questions with regards to how user data are used, stored, and protected. Given its origination with the for-profit healthcare industry, its viability as a democratic social network for adolescent health literacy education remains to be seen. Nevertheless, it illustrates the power and potential of using transmedia to cultivate positive health-related behaviors among teenagers.

MEDIA LITERACY: ASKING CRITICAL QUESTIONS

Health is not solely determined by what or how much food or drink we consume. It is also determined in part by how much energy we expend or, in other words, to what extent we actively use our bodies. Similarly, health literacy is not exclusively based on how many nutrition labels we can decipher or how many health facts we can accrue. It is also determined in part by how we actively, socially, and civically engage across a variety of media forms. In other words, it's insufficient to just be consumers. We must be creators as well.

Just as there exist within the United States many different perspectives on how to cultivate health among teenagers, there also exist many different perspectives on how to cultivate media literacy among teenagers. Not everyone agrees to what extent young people are active participants in the process. Generally defined, media literacy is the ability to access, analyze, evaluate, create, reflect, and act on information across a variety of forms.[26] Media literate individuals must be able to deeply engage with all forms of media to discern between what is inferential (interpretation) and what is observable (fact). Explaining the difference between interpretation and fact can occur by comparing evidence-based scientific research about a pharmaceutical drug with a marketing tactic for selling that drug to consumers. While neither is a pure example of interpretation nor fact, the value lies in the distinction between the two methods of communication.

The more challenging task of media literacy and health is to bridge the gap between knowledge and action or behavior. The connector is *reflection*—obtaining a personal understanding of the importance of critical analysis (of media messages, forms, and technologies) and what it reveals.[27] A media literate approach to health begins with a deeper understanding of the interpretation, constructions, ownership, values, and language of media messages. The following five essential questions can serve as a starting point for reflective discussion with teenagers.

How Do Users Interpret Health Messages?

All media supply youth with powerful symbolic material from which to negotiate meaning and to establish an identity in the context of the world around them. Meaning does not reside in the text itself, but is a product of the interaction between text and audience. There are mixed messages about where the power or agency resides. A highly protectionist stance ascribes power primarily to media institutions and messages. In contrast, an extreme stance of empowerment might mistake an individual as self-constructing their own media reality and free from outside influence. A balanced approach acknowledges the transactional nature between individuals and groups and the media constructions and messages.

Audiences interpret meaning based on situational elements such as geography, culture, race, age, class, gender, time of day, and the context in which they interact with the medium. Various media forms resonate in different ways, depending upon the experiences, values, and knowledge that audiences bring to it. For example, research indicates that black and Hispanic teens watch significantly more TV than white teens. One study found black teens viewed more than five hours more of TV per week and Hispanic teens nearly two hours more compared to their white peers.[28] The same study revealed male teens play video games nine hours more per week than their female counterparts and watch one hour more of TV per week. Other research suggests that TV is the "least socially elite" medium, and the Internet is the "most socially elite."[29] These findings are fodder for discussion among teens. What may emerge from reflective discussion are ways in which the uses of media technologies intertwine with sociocultural preferences, socioeconomic disparities, gender roles, and racial and ethnic differences.

Although all audiences differ in their perceptions, understandings, and reactions to media, the key to media literacy in this case is to educate teens to be aware of their own subjectivity as well as the subjectivity of other audiences. Likewise, facilitators of these critical questions should pose questions without supplying answers or alternative ideologies. Educators should steward teens toward authentic, observation-based answers that meaningfully lead them to their own contextualized definition of health.

How Is Health Constructed *through Mass Media?*

While teens make meaning and construct their own reality, there are also powerful institutional forces at play that shape thoughts, attitudes, and behaviors. Media are neither reality nor windows to the world. Instead, they are carefully constructed products that represent a particular view of actual people, places, events, and ideas. A media literate person is aware that many decisions are made in the construction of each media product and that even the most realistic images represent an interpretation of reality. Not only are Hollywood films highly constructed, but so are newspaper headlines, nature documentaries, and pharmaceutical advertisements. Teens might ask of a health message, "To what extent is this medium/message representative of my reality?" Research indicates that formalized media literacy education/classroom instruction enables high school students to understand media structure and influence—including the construction of reality in TV commercials.[30]

An understanding of the constructed nature of mediated messages extends to health messages as well. Over the last few years, product manufacturers have added their own nutrition labels on the front of packaging on store shelves to increase the prominence of the nutrition labeling that is generally located on the side or back of the package. Manufacturers use terms such as *natural* and *organic* to catch the consumer's attention and to associate their product with health. Although "organic" foods have slightly lower pesticide residue, they are nutritionally not that much different than nonorganic foods.[31]

Health-related terms are frequently used on products that are not technically healthy and compel the consumer to bypass more careful and critical review of the ingredients label. Melanie Warner, author of *Pandora's Lunchbox*, laments this technique of "leanwashing" processed foods to portray them as being of higher nutritional value than they actually are. She notes that placing labels such as "high in fiber" and "good source of vitamins" on sugary cereal "doesn't make a food good for us, only less bad."[32] The rhetoric surrounding "organic" foods can be just as misleading as fast-food advertising. Current food marketing messages that claim to aid digestion (e.g., probiotic yogurt) and to boost brainpower (omega-3) may not be much different from the snake oil claims of the early twentieth century. The high amount of sugar, sweeteners, artificial colors, flavorings, and preservatives contained in these products render the nutritional claims highly suspect.

Learning the techniques of advertising and facilitating a reflective understanding of rhetorical devices has historically been key to successfully mitigating the negative health effects of alcohol and tobacco[33] as well as combatting unrealistic body image among females.[34] Decoding the carefully constructed language of nutrition labels and gaining a deeper understanding of their real health implications is essential.

How Are Media Languages Used To Construct Health?

Each media form has its own specific language or set of codes and conventions, such as editing, hyperlinking, sequencing, timing, or framing as examples. These media techniques impact the message conveyed. Marshall McLuhan is known for his popular statement, "the medium *is* the message" or that the technological form heavily influences and in some cases overrides the message content. Often the audience or user is oblivious to the impact of the technological form. For example, an obese teen might be able to decode the persuasive techniques of a junk food commercial on TV. Yet, he or she may be unaware that the sedentary act of TV viewing may also contribute to obesity.

Technical knowledge and proficiency are important components of media literacy. Along similar lines, having cooking skills is positively associated with more healthful eating habits.[35] Yet Americans are cooking less frequently and overall food preparation skills are in decline. Additionally, more people are reading, browsing, and tuning in to food media such as the Food Network, *Iron Chef*, and *MasterChef*. Yet the primary purpose of these shows is to keep the viewer's attention rather than encourage him/her to cook.[36] As such, these media forms may run counter to rather than in conjunction with healthy behaviors. Yet research indicates that activating knowledge about the production/preparation of food itself *and the production of media texts about food* strengthens a viewer's capacity for critical analysis.[37] It's not just food preparation skills that are essential to health literacy—so are media production skills.

What Values Are Associated with Health through and across Media?

The language of newspapers, magazines, television, and the Internet use shortcuts to meaning, also known as *stereotyping*, which may oppress certain groups of people. Questions to ask of each media message are: "Whose story is told?" "Whose story is left out?" At the same time, the health information that news media circulate through various channels may convey a set of values not shared by the audiences in desperate need of the information. This is a major challenge among scientists and journalists who don't necessarily agree on what health information is "newsworthy."[38] Translating complex research into digestible news for the public is a difficult task and the field of journalism is struggling to provide better training in this area.[39] It is also increasingly more difficult to discern between public relations, advertising, and authentic news reporting.

Corporations literally construct alternate identities or front groups to gain favor with the public and in some cases conceal their true purpose. They then appeal to the needs and values of those whom they want to persuade. A well-known front group for the tobacco, restaurant, and alcoholic beverage industries is the Center for Consumer Freedom that began in the 1990s with funding by the tobacco company Phillip Morris. The Center claims as its mission defending "the freedom to buy what we want, eat what we want, drink what we want, and raise our children as we see fit." They demonize their opposition as "self-anointed 'food police,' health campaigners, trial lawyers, personal-finance do-gooders, animal-rights misanthropes, and meddling bureaucrats."[40] Other examples of front groups include the Alliance to Feed the Future, which represents the interests of agribusiness and trade groups, and the U.S. Farmers and Ranchers Alliance, which represents the interests of Monsanto (the producer of genetically engineered seed) and the National Pork Board.

Two of the techniques that front groups employ are *astroturfing*, or pretending to represent the public interests, and *scaremongering*, or preying on people's fear.[41] This was the case with a 2012 California ballot initiative (Proposition 37) that would require packagers to label foods containing genetically modified organisms (GMOs). Democratic Voter's Choice (a for-profit Slate Mailer Organization) circulated flyers opposing Proposition 37, citing "special interest loopholes" and warning voters of increased grocery bills if the measure passed.[42] Despite the motive of Proposition 37 to achieve more transparency in labeling GMOs in food packages, Democratic Voter's Choice spent US$46 million to convince California voters that the initiative would harm them economically. Not surprisingly, Proposition 37 was defeated.

Who Owns the Media Constructions of Health?

It is no surprise that media messages can never be neutral since they are owned, produced, distributed, and/or used by individuals or groups with a bias, point of view, political agenda, and/or economic motive. These individuals or institutions have historical and social contexts that may be concealed from the general public. For example, more than half of all food sales in the United States are controlled by the ten largest food companies.[43] Food activist Michael Pollan explains that when we walk through the supermarket, we may see a variety of choices, but it is ultimately an illusion of diversity. Instead there are only a few companies that manipulate a few crops. Pollan notes that much of it is just "clever rearrangements of corn."[44] Individuals are thus faced with the extraordinarily difficult challenge of navigating a food system dominated by highly processed foods and drinks that are controlled by powerful transnational corporations.

There is power in asking questions about media ownership as well as food ownership. Raj Patel in *Stuffed and Starved* raises critical questions about the history, production, and marketing of coffee—and its worldwide impact. Instead of admonishing teenagers to avoid coffee, we would do well to facilitate critical questioning: How is coffee made and by whom? Where are coffee beans grown? Who buys coffee? Who gets paid? What is the cultural meaning of coffee in U.S. culture? What is the meaning of coffee to farmers in Uganda, Vietnam, and South Africa? Media literacy education that scaffolds teens' critical questioning of food ownership yields real answers that resonate with their own understanding and experience.[45]

Institutional elements from production to distribution influence media content as well as audience perceptions of that content. Some food and beverage companies use science to generate sales and profits at the expense of directly addressing the real health concerns. An example of this is the recent "Coming Together" anti-obesity marketing campaign of Coca-Cola. In line with the current call for reducing sugar consumption, "Coming Together," promotes the company's increased production of no-calorie and low-calorie drinks. Coca-Cola claims they have decreased the number of calories consumed by school-aged children in school by 90 percent since 2004. This can easily be accomplished by increasing the sales of Dasani water, also owned by Coca-Cola. The campaign slogan is "All calories count, no matter where they come from," but that does not say that Coca-Cola products have little, if any, nutritional value.[46]

It is essential to acknowledge the constructed, owned, mediated, and technologized nature of health-related information. The commercialization of health communication is of particular concern. The heightened concern about industrial influence is such that the United Nations Non-Communicable Diseases Action Group (UNNCDAG) has called for a new discipline of study to investigate industrial diseases "and the transnational corporations that drive them."[47] The UNNCDAG recommends that researchers and educators *not* accept funding from tobacco, alcohol, and processed food and drink industries, or even those with which they affiliate.

MORPHING ANALYSIS INTO ACTION

It is quite possible that a person can survive on the basics of health literacy (e.g., the ability to read a food product label). However, without the ability to analyze the information for one's own needs or that of a family member it is disempowering and even hazardous.[48] Similarly, a person is not fully media literate if they can only decode or deconstruct a media text without acquiring the ability to compose a text for themselves—whether it be through oral, print, audio, visual, or object media forms. A media literate approach to health is more than the acquisition of critical knowledge about health; one must also apply that knowledge in one's surroundings.

From a cultural studies perspective, mass media can serve as a facilitator of top-down social, economic, and political oppression. However, a liberatory approach to mass media views them as tools for democratic practices that resist oppression. Public schools are contexts where bureaucratic constraints and democratic ideals collide, but the result ideally is the refinement of interpersonal and cognitive skills through learning how to civilly dissent and debate. Based on the current social, political, and economic needs of American culture, such discursive practices must be woven throughout the high school curriculum as methodology as well as curriculum content.

Classrooms can be sites to explore thoughtful, logical, critical interpretations that are grounded in discovery and the use of evidence. Problematizing the issues and engaging in classroom dialogue about health messages as constructed, owned, value-laden, yet still open to audience interpretation, can empower teenagers outside the classroom to intentionally act upon their knowledge as opposed to merely avoiding or reacting to information.[49] Telling teens what to do or how to achieve good health is ineffective. Rather, fostering authentic yet mediated experiences that further their cognitive and social development, honor their free agency, and magnify their unique perspectives is a more pedagogically sound approach. At the same time, teachers who are trained in the concepts and skills of media literacy education require a year or more of consistent classroom practice to be able to facilitate authentic discussions wherein students discover concepts for themselves.[50]

New technologies have evoked a higher level of technical skills from teens. At the same time, these new technologies have created an urgent need for critical thinking skills grounded in evidence-based observation, analysis, evaluation, production, communication, and social action. While critical media health literacy is a set of individual skills, it cannot be accomplished without societal structures that allow individuals to conscientiously exercise their agency.

NOTES

1. Victoria J. Rideout, Ulla G. Foehr, and Donald F. Roberts, *Generation M2: Media in the Lives of 8- to 18-Year-old*. Washington, DC: Kaiser Family Foundation, 2010.
2. Catherine Donaldson-Evans, "Schools Make Rules for Cell Phone No- nos," Fox News, September 23, 2004, http://www.foxnews.com/story/0,2933,133208,00.html.
3. Mizuko Ito, *Hanging Out, Messing Around, and Geeking Out*. Cambridge, MA: MIT Press, 2013.
4. Amanda Lenhart, Kristen Purcell, Aaron Smith, and Kathryn Zickuhr, *Social Media and Mobile Internet Use among Teens and Young Adults*. Washington, DC: Pew Internet & American Life Project, 2011, 23.
5. Ulla G. Foehr, *Media Multitasking among American Youth: Prevalence, Predictors and Pairings*. Menlo Park, CA: Kaiser Family Foundation, 2006.
6. Vanessa Domine, "From Savvy Consumer to Responsible Citizen: Teen Perspectives of Advertising in the Classroom," *Journal of Media Literacy* 51, no. 2 (2004): 45–52.
7. Amanda Lenhart, Lee Rainie, and O. Lewis, *Teenage Life Online: The Rise of the Instant-Message Generation and the Internet's Impact on Friendships and Family Relationships*. Washington, DC: Kaiser Family Foundation, 2001.
8. Sonia Livingstone and Moira Bovill, eds., *Children and Their Changing Media Environment*. London: Lawrence Erlbaum Associates, 2001.
9. Federal Trade Commission, "FTC Announces Settlements with Web Sites that Collected Children's Personal Data without Parental Permission," April 19, 2001, http://www.ftc.gov/news-events/press-releases/2001/04/ftc-announces-settlements-web-sites-collected-childrens-personal.
10. Federal Trade Commission, "FTC Receives Largest COPP Civil Penalties to Date in Settlements with Mrs. Fields Cookies and Hershey Foods," February 27, 2003, http://www.ftc.gov/news-events/press-releases/2003/02/ftc-receives-largest-coppa-civil-penalties-date-settlements-mrs.
11. Columbia University Health, "What Is the Mission of Go Ask Alice!?" http://goaskalice.columbia.edu/about-us.
12. Columbia University Health, "Go Ask Alice! History," http://goaskalice.columbia.edu/go-ask-alice-history.
13. Victor John Strecher, "Internet Methods for Delivering Behavioral and Health-Related Interventions (eHealth)," *Annual Review of Clinical Psychology* 3 (2007): 53–76.
14. Suzanne Suggs, "A 10-Year Retrospective of Research in New Technologies for Health Communication," *Journal of Health Communication* 11 (2006): 61–74.
15. Erica Weintraub Austin, Bruce E. Pinkleton, Bruce W. Austin, and Rebecca Van de Vord, "The Relationships of Information Efficacy and Media Literacy Skills to Knowledge and Self-Efficacy for Health-Related Decision Making," *Journal of American College Health* 60, no. 8 (2012): 548–54, doi: 10.1080/07448481.2012.726302.
16. Mary Grace Flaherty, "Health Literacy: An Overview of an Emerging Field," *San Jose State University School of Library and Information Science Student Research Journal* 1, no. 2 (2011), http://scholarworks.sjsu.edu/slissrj/vol1/iss2/4.
17. Renee Hobbs, *Digital and Media Literacy: A Plan of Action*. Washington, DC: Aspen Institute, 2010, http://www.knightcomm.org/digital-and-media-literacy-a-plan-of-action.
18. Nicholas A. Christakis and James H. Fowler, "Social Network Sensors for Early Detection of Contagious Outbreaks," *PLoS ONE* 5, no. 9 (2010): e12948, http://dx.doi.org/10.1371/journal.pone.0012948.
19. Charles W. Schmidt, "Trending Now: Using Social Media to Predict and Track Disease Outbreaks," *Environmental Health Perspectives* 120, no. 1 (2012): A30–A33.
20. Every Child Stronger, Every Life Longer. "Fitnessgram Program Overview—Teachers," http://everychildstronger.org/?page_id=474. Retrieved September 18, 2014.
21. Alissa Quart, "The Body-Data Craze," *Newsweek*, June 26, 2013, http://www.thedailybeast.com/newsweek/2013/06/26/the-body-data-craze.html.

22. Rush University Medical Center, "Two Chicago School Cafeterias to Use Technology to Create a Healthy Eating 'Report Card' on Students' Food Choices and Eating Habits to Help Prevent Childhood Obesity" [press release], August 21, 2014, http://www.newswise.com/articles/two-chicago-school-cafeterias-to-use-technology-to-create-a-healthy-eating-report-card-on-students-food-choices-and-eating-habits-to-help-prevent-childhood-obesity.

23. Elaine Quiter, "T2x: Educating Youth on Health & Wellness Using Social Media," 2012, http://publichealth.lacounty.gov/nut/lacollab/Docs/May%202013/T2X%20Site%20and%20Campaign%20Overview%20-%20Endowment_May2013v2.pdf.

24. *Club Episode 1: New Meat*, written and directed by Kevin Blake, produced by Lori Nelson and Skyler Jackson, ENCOMPASS Production, 2012.

25. Judy Temes, "Health Net and UCLA Expand Social Media Program," *San Fernando Valley Business Journal*, January 11, 2012, §4, http://sfvbj.com/news/2012/jan/11/health-net-and-ucla-expand-social-media-program/.

26. National Association for Media Literacy Education (NAMLE), "Media Literacy Defined," 2007, http://namle.net/publications/media-literacy-definitions/.

27. Cynthia L. Scheibe and Faith Rogow, *The Teacher's Guide to Media Literacy: Critical Thinking in a Multimedia World*. Thousand Oaks, CA: Corwin Press, 2011.

28. Melanie Burleson Richards, "Mass Media's Relationship with Adolescents' Values and Behavior: A Theory of Mediated Valueflection," *Sociology Dissertations*. Paper 49, 2010, 57.

29. Richards, "Mass Media's Relationship with Adolescents' Values and Behavior," 63.

30. George Sebastian Vallocheril and William J. Thorn, "Media Literacy Education for Adolescents: Testing and Integrated Theory of Media Literacy," January 1, 1997, *Dissertations (1962–2010) Access via Proquest Digital Dissertations*. Paper AAI9823991. http://epublications.marquette.edu/dissertations/AAI9823991.

31. Crystal Smith-Spangler, Margaret L. Brandeau, Grace E. Hunter, J. Clay Bavinger, Maren Pearson, Paul J. Eschbach, Vandana Sundaram, Hau Liu, Patricia Schirmer, Christopher Stave, Ingram Olkin, and Dena M. Bravata, "Are Organic Foods Safer or Healthier Than Conventional Alternatives?: A Systematic Review," *Annals of Internal Medicine* 157, no. 5 (2012): 348–66,doi: 10.7326/0003-4819-157-5-201209040-00007.

32. Spangler et al., "Are Organic Foods Safer."

33. Erica Weintraub Austin and Kristine Kay Johnson, "Effects of General and Alcohol-Specific Media Literacy Training on Children's Decision Making about Alcohol." *Journal of Health Communication* 2 (1997): 17–42.

34. Niva Piran, Michael P. Levine, and Lori M. Irving, "Go Girls! Media Literacy, Activism, and Advocacy Project," *Healthy Weight Journal* 6 (2000): 89–90.

35. Elizabeth Dowler and Clair Calvert, "Nutrition and Diet in Lone-Parent Families in London." London: Family Policy Studies Centre, 1995.

36. Tina L. Peterson, "Exploring Baseline Food-Media Literacy of Adult Women," *Journal of Media Literacy Education* 4 (2012): 3.

37. Peterson, "Exploring Baseline Food-Media Literacy of Adult Women," 3.

38. National Research Council, *The Future of the Public's Health in the 21st Century*. Washington, DC: National Academies Press, 2003, 310.

39. B. Kees, "Newsroom Training: Where's the Investment? Survey Context, Analysis and Commentary," November 22, 2002, The Poynter Institute, http://www.poynter.org/content/content_view.asp?id=10841. Accessed July 1, 2013.

40. Center for Consumer Freedom, "About Us: What Is the Center for Consumer Freedom?" https://www.consumerfreedom.com/about/.

41. Michele Simon, *The Best Public Relations That Money Can Buy: A Guide to Industry Front Groups*. Washington, DC: Center for Food Safety, 2013. http://www.centerforfoodsafety.org/files/front_groups_final_84531.pdf.

42. California Right To Know, "Front Groups Against Prop 37: Foes of Honest Labeling Pose as Fake Cops and Phony Democrats to Trick Voters" [press release], November 5, 2012, http://www.carighttoknow.org/foes_of_honest_labeling.

43. Thomas Lyson and Annalisa Lewis Raymer, "Stalking the Wily Multinational: Power and Control in the US Food System," *Agriculture and Human Values* 17 (2000): 199–208.

44. *Food, Inc.* [documentary film]. Directed by Robert Kenner. Participant Media & River Road Entertainment, 2008: 17:33.

45. Hannah Wallace, "In High Schools, A Critical Lens on Food," *New York Times*, October 26, 2011. A26.

46. Qing Yang, "Gain Weight by 'Going Diet?' Artificial Sweetners and the Neurobiology of Sugar Cravings," *Yale Journal of Biology and Medicine* 83 (2010): 101–8.

47. Rob Moodie, David Stuckler, Carlos Monteiro, Nick Sheron, Bruce Neal, Thaksaphon Thamarangsi, Paul Lincoln, and Sally Casswell, "Profits and Pandemics: Prevention of Harmful Effects of Tobacco, Alcohol, and Ultra-Processed Food and Drink Industries," *Lancet* 381 (2013): 676.

48. Lawrence St. Leger, "Schools, Health Literacy and Public Health: Possibilities and Challenges," *Health Promotion International* 16 (2001): 198.

49. David R. Buchanan, "Beyond Positivism: Humanistic Perspectives on Theory and Research in Health Education," *Health Education Research: Theory & Practice* 13, no. 3 (1998): 444.

50. Elizabeth Thoman and Tessa Jolls, "Media Literacy Education: Lessons from the Center for Media Literacy," in *Media Literacy: Transforming Curriculum and Teaching—104th Yearbook of the National Society for the Study of Education*, ed. Gretchen Schwarz, and Pamela Unruh Brown, 180–205. Malden, MA: Blackwell Publishing.

FOUR

The Politics of Adolescent Health

On May 10, 2002, in Sao Paulo, Brazil, the World Health Organization (WHO) encouraged member states to establish an "Annual Move for Health Day" to promote physical activity as essential for health and well-being. The annual celebration was linked to broader initiatives to promote physical activity and healthy lifestyles throughout the year. In 2005, the focus of the Move for Health Day was *supportive environments*, to enable more people to participate and achieve the recommended half an hour per day of moderately intense physical activity.

The WHO noted "active living also positively contributes to economic prosperity and social cohesion in cities. Taking part in physical activity increases opportunities for socialization, networking and cultural identity."[1] Move for Health Day appealed to multiculturalism and economic prosperity, and the WHO called for strong national and local political commitment and support for similar initiatives within member states. The U.S. government responded with a renewed commitment to health and physical education, but not without controversy.

LET'S MOVE TO PEPSI

On February 9, 2010, U.S. president Barak Obama created the Task Force on Childhood Obesity. That same day, First Lady Michelle Obama kicked off her *Let's Move!* campaign, a "comprehensive initiative" dedicated to "solving the challenge of obesity within a generation, so that children born today will grow up healthier and able to pursue their dreams."[2] The campaign was a coalescence of existing and new initiatives: healthier food in school, increased physical activity among children, and the implementation of better food labeling.

Let's Move! was slick in its public relations approach. Michelle Obama recruited Beyoncé Knowles Carter as the celebrity spokesperson. The theme song of the campaign was a remix of "Get Me Bodied" by Beyoncé and Swizz Beatz. The title and lyrics were changed to "Move Your Body," and the music video was filmed in a school cafeteria featuring Beyoncé dancing with teenagers. Beyoncé made personal appearances alongside Michelle Obama at inner-city schools across the country and touted the benefits of exercise.

At first, *Let's Move!* had the qualities of a successful public health campaign. It magnified the research findings that children are six times more likely to change their physical activity level to match that of their friends instead of maintaining their own physical activity level.[3] The campaign also had the leadership of the first lady of the United States, who has a high favorability rating, particularly among black and Hispanic populations. The marketing power exponentially increased with the added celebrity endorsement of Beyoncé, one of the most powerful popular cultural icons, particularly among young black females. Both Michelle Obama and later the president of the United States publicly confessed that Beyoncé is a role model for their two daughters.[4]

The positive health messages of *Let's Move* were diluted, however, in 2012 after Beyoncé signed a US$50 million endorsement deal with Pepsi-Co. As brand ambassador, Beyoncé's face appeared on soda cans and in Superbowl ads. PepsiCo sponsored Beyoncé's concert tour and supplied money "to support the singer's chosen creative projects." Critics pointed to the hypocrisy of her simultaneous involvement with *Let's Move* and Pepsi-Cola, given PepsiCo's aggressive marketing to black Americans, a U.S. population at higher risk than others for obesity. The Beyoncé controversy came to a head in September 2013 when she teamed with her husband, rapper Jay-Z (also the co-brand director of Budweiser), to perform a Labor Day "Budweiser Made in America" concert in Philadelphia. The timing of the Budweiser concert performance did not bode well for *Let's Move!* as September is also National Childhood Obesity Awareness Month—a designation made by President Obama in 2011.

The Beyoncé controversy also called attention to PepsiCo's American roots of marketing to black communities in the 1940s and what historians label as preying on the financial needs of "negro markets." Grace Elizabeth Hale writes in "When Jim Crow Drank Coke," "Black fashion models appeared in Pepsi ads in black publications, and special point-of-purchase displays appeared in stores patronized by African-Americans. The company hired Duke Ellington as a spokesman."[5] The Beyoncé controversy was reminiscent of PepsiCo's history of racially motivated marketing.

UNDER THE INFLUENCE

In 2013, the Center for Science in the Public Interest (CSPI) released the report *Selfish Giving: How the Soda Industry Uses Philanthropy to Sweeten Its Profits*. The report called attention to the philanthropic strategies that soda companies employ to garner public trust and goodwill to increase brand awareness and brand loyalty.[6] Known as *philanthro-marketing*, corporations use this as a means of increasing product sales.

One example is Pepsi Refresh, a website launched in 2010.[7] The online campaign invites people, businesses, and nonprofit organizations to submit grant-funding ideas that "will have a positive impact on the world." The categories for ideas include health, arts and culture, food and shelter, the planet, neighborhoods, and education. Over the course of a month, website visitors vote on their favorite idea and then finalists receive grant money. PepsiCo distributes up to US$1.3 million each month. The social media angle allows for crowdsourcing of support for ideas that are, to a certain extent, socially activist oriented. Yet, PepsiCo ultimately decides where to put their grant money and is therefore defining the agenda for social activism.[8]

A current marketing strategy is to link a brand to health and wellness rather than to illness and obesity. Marketers reframe the food and beverage industry as part of the solution ("part of a healthy diet") rather than as part of the problem. As an example, in 2011 McDonald's announced menu modifications with the promise that by 2020 the chain will reduce added sugar, saturated fat, and calories through varied portion sizes and "reformulations" to reduce sodium an average of 15 percent across its national menu by 2015. This approach appears as industry self-regulation or a contribution to the common good; yet, the fundamental motive is to increase product sales by riding the rhetorical wave of health.

Soda companies also reframe the health problem as a lack of exercise and therefore the solution is to increase individual physical activity. This deflects attention away from claims that link sugary beverages to obesity and diabetes. As an example, Coca-Cola invested in the exercise program "Step with It!" to associate Coke in schools with healthy activity. As the oldest corporate supporter of the Olympics, Coca-Cola currently spins the narrative of "proper hydration" rather than drinking less soda. In 2009, Coca-Cola donated US$600,000 to the American Academy of Family Physicians (AAFP) to support the development of the FamilyDoctor.org website. On the topic of sugar drinks, the website employs Coca-Cola's hydration narrative rather than avoidance.[9]

Although criticized by the American public, corporate lobbying has been a constitutionally protected practice (under freedom of speech) in the United States. Lobbying has significantly increased since the 1970s, and although there are currently more than twelve thousand registered lobbyists in Washington, D.C., there are likely close to one hundred thousand as they use increasingly surreptitious "underground" methods, including nonregistration.[10]

The top two lobbying clients in 2014 were Coca-Cola and PepsiCo, respectively. Lobbying is highly effective in shaping government policy. For example, in 2009 Congress considered a soda tax, and the beverage industry spent more than US$40 million in lobbying against it. This expenditure was more than eight times the US$4.8 million they had spent lobbying the year prior. In 2010 the FDA's draft of the Affordable Care Act required calorie information to be posted in a wide range of venues, including movie theaters, lunch wagons, bowling alleys, trains, and airlines. However, corporate lobbying led the FDA to propose rules that only covered fast-food chain restaurants and vending machines.[11]

Given the correlation between sugary drinks, obesity, and poor health, health advocates support the elimination of sugary drinks from eligibility under the Supplemental Nutrition Assistance Program (SNAP), formerly known as the Food Stamps program. Yet, the Food Research and Action Center (FRAC) and Feeding America oppose this move. This opposition is most likely linked to the influence of corporate sponsors for FRAC's 2012 annual dinner that included PepsiCo, the American Beverage Association, Nestle USA, and Mars, Inc.[12]

Organizations that appear to be beneficial to public health are under undue influence through their association with industries that may run contrary in purpose. For example, the American Academy of Pediatrics in 2012 established the Institute for Healthy Childhood Weight to provide pediatricians, families, and communities with evidence-based resources to help prevent and treat childhood obesity. The founding sponsor that enabled the launch of the institute is Nestle, the largest revenue generating food company on the world. The multinational company's holdings include baby food, bottled water, breakfast cereals, coffee and tea, confectionery, dairy products, ice cream, frozen food, pet foods, and snacks.

In 2012 controversy erupted when Nestle co-branded their candy bars with Girl Scouts, stirring criticism from public health advocates, including the CSPI, that Nestle was in violation of its commitment to not market to children under twelve.[13] The CSPI also reported that the Nestle candy bars contain more calories, more saturated fat, and more sugar than the actual Girl Scout cookies.

In 2011 the United Nations convened on the cause of preventing non-communicable diseases (NCDs) in low-income and middle-income countries. The committee called for coordinated action across multiple sectors, including cooperation with the private sector and industry. However, some public health officials conclude that industry should have no involvement in forming national or international policy.[14] One of the concerns is the financial and institutional relationship between public health researchers and industry. Such relationships compromise research findings.[15] Yet due to decreased funding, the WHO is now engaging in "voluntary" partnerships with industries, which includes accepting money from Coca-Cola, Nestle, and other manufacturers of sugary foods and drinks.[16]

GOVERNMENT REGULATION

Public health advocates have both praised and condemned former New York mayor Michael Bloomberg for his anti-obesity policies. Among his enacted policies are calorie disclosures in chain restaurants, banning the use of trans fats, limiting smoking in public places, and limiting the calorie and sugar contents of food sold in school vending machines. In May 2012, Bloomberg ignited controversy by attempting to ban the sale of sugary beverages exceeding 16 ounces in restaurants, movie theaters, and street carts. The measure would not have applied to diet sodas, fruit juices, dairy-based drinks, or alcoholic beverages and would not extend to beverages sold in grocery or convenience stores.

While the sugary beverage ban gained traction initially, it was eventually overturned based on jurisdiction: New York City did not have the power to ban supersized sugar drinks everywhere, but only in establishments regulated by the Health Department. This meant that a person could buy a supersized beverage at a convenience store but not in a restaurant. Businesses impacted by the ban claimed they were victims of unequal treatment. And while the financial interests of New York City businesses (both small and large) were ultimately protected, it is difficult to discern if the overturn of the ban was a win for consumer rights or a victory for the beverage industry, or both.

Those who oppose taxpayer-funded campaigns against sugary beverages and junk food argue that it is not the role of the federal government to regulate consumer habits on products that are considered safe by the FDA. Yet government regulation can play a significant role in consumer behavior. Dr. Marion Nestle, nutrition professor and author of *Food Politics*, points out the value in a regulatory approach and cites studies of the effects of menu labeling:

> Not everyone pays attention, but those who do are more likely to reduce their calorie purchases. . . . Kids living in states where schools don't sell junk food are not as overweight. The benefits of the approaches shown in these studies may appear small, but together they offer hope that current trends can be reversed.[17]

The sugary beverage controversy is microcosmic of a larger polarization of public opinion about the corporatization of communities. Opponents to government regulation maintained that consumers should be free to choose and that educating Americans to critically consume media (rather than controlling what they eat and drink) is the answer. While some cities are proposing bans and taxes on soda, others are signing exclusive beverage contracts. In 2012, Miami Beach officials signed a ten-year contract with Coca-Cola; and officials from Ocean City, Maryland, and Dayton, Ohio, both signed five-year contracts with Coca-Cola to be the "Official Soft Drink" sponsor of these cities.

Government intervention on behalf of the health of individuals is indeed a slippery slope. In 2011, an eight-year-old boy in Ohio was taken from his family and placed in foster care after county case workers worked with the mother unsuccessfully for a year to try to control the boy's weight (which exceeded two hundred pounds). It was the first time a child was removed from a home for strictly a weight-related issue.[18] This raises significant questions about the authority of the federal, state, and local governments over personal health issues and whether or not future risk of health problems warrants a child to be separated from his or her family. Moreover, it is paradoxical if the federal government on one hand usurps parental authority while at the same time allowing the food and beverage industry to advertise unhealthy food and beverages to minors.

The default approach of the U.S. and other governments that comprise the United Nations is industry-operated, voluntary self-regulation. However, this often leads to procrastination and delay on the part of industry in an effort to avoid regulation.[19] A 2013 UN Non-Communicable Diseases Working Group stated:

> As an alternative to regulatory measures, alcohol and food industries promote ineffective individually-targeted information and educational approaches, and sometimes employ counter-productive covert marketing. Their social-marketing campaigns place responsibility for the purchasing decision on the individual, and in doing so, separate these choices from the circumstances in which they are made. The media regularly emphasise [sic] personal choice and responsibility and convey government intervention as coercive and oppressive.[20]

Among the suggested strategies from the working group is to put constant and direct pressure on industry to change by making harmful practices obvious and continually raising public awareness of the negative actions of industry.

THE POLITICAL BATTLEFIELD OF THE SCHOOL CAFETERIA

Health politics may ring the loudest in the context of public school cafeterias, where the debate continues over U.S. Department of Agriculture (USDA) school lunch and breakfast guidelines. The 2010 Healthy Hunger-Free Kids Act reauthorized the Child Nutrition Bill and instructed the USDA to develop higher nutrition standards for school breakfasts and lunches based on recommendations from the Institute of Medicine. These included serving more fruits, vegetables, whole grains, and lower-fat dairy products.

In 2012 the USDA officially approved the guidelines that essentially doubled the amount of fruit served at breakfast; increased the quantity of vegetables in lunches; and required serving dark green and orange vegetables. The guidelines also placed limits on the amount of salt and calories and the phasing-in of whole grains only by 2014. Schools can still serve chocolate milk, but it has to be lowfat or nonfat. For the first time, the USDA allows tofu to be counted as a protein in school lunches; there is a cap of nine servings of grain per week; and a maximum number of calories are allowed per meal.

There were some additional changes in the USDA guidelines due to political pressure from food lobbyists between 2010 and when they were officially released in 2012. Congress intervened, and the result was an altered set of USDA school nutrition guidelines that gave schools greater flexibility: Tomato sauce on pizza is allowed to count as a vegetable serving, based on its nutritional content. Potatoes (French fries) can be served as a vegetable but limited to two times per week. These allowances were fodder for criticism and even mockery in the popular press of the undue influence of industry and even Congress upon U.S. Food and Drug Administration (FDA) guidelines.

Dr. Marion Nestle observed that food companies claim congressional micromanagement as infringing upon their right to sell (unhealthy) food to children. The industry pressure is also felt at the local level, as beverage contracts impact the implementation of nutritional guidelines. For example, in 2011, the Los Angeles Unified School District (LAUSD) in a proactive move banned flavored milk in their cafeteria. However, they allowed orange juice, which contains just as much sugar and even less protein. This choice may have been influenced by the exclusive beverage contract between LAUSD and Coca-Cola, the distributor of Minute Maid orange juice.

The restriction on calories (750–850 calories for high school lunches) generated intense debate among teenagers who argue they are left hungry. In 2012, teenagers from Kansas to Wisconsin staged protests against the new school lunches through Twitter campaigns, boycotts, and filming videos to garner attention for their cause. Teens argued they require more calories because they burn more through sports and other activities. Advocacy groups also questioned the calorie limit, noting that poverty and obesity are intertwined and therefore the calorie limit should not be imposed for schools that receive Title I funding. While there is a scientific rationale behind the changes in the USDA nutritional guidelines, it is not readily transparent to the students (or educators) who are ultimately responsible for making healthy choices. As such, there is an opportunity for the school cafeteria to serve as a classroom as well.

Maximizing Nutritional Value

Since 1985, federal law has prohibited the sale of foods of "minimal nutritional value" during public school mealtimes. The federal standard defines unhealthy foods as those with less than 5 percent of the recommended daily intake of eight key nutrients. Soda, hard candies, cookies, and gum fall into the unhealthy category. Parents nationwide broadly support the creation of strong guidelines on food sold in school vending machines, but leave wide open bake sales and fund-raisers. California and Massachusetts have been at the forefront of legislating strict guidelines for snack foods sold in schools. In 2011, fourteen New York City high schools tested vending machines that sold fresh fruit (mango, watermelon, and pineapple) and vegetables (carrots and celery). Current USDA federal guidelines require that vending machines must stock foods of maximum nutritional value, such as whole wheat crackers, granola bars, and dried fruits.

Even snacks defined as "healthy" need a sales pitch, however. To this end, Human Healthy Vending designed a machine with a digital LCD screen that streams images of a Kashi granola bar with the video message: "Hey, looking for a sustained energy snack to get you through practice?" The CEO stated, "You cannot just take a standard vending machine, throw graphics on it, put some healthier options in there and expect everything to work out perfectly," so he employs digital messages along with free samples and contests to increase average monthly sales.[21] This raises the questions, "What, if any, types of advertising and point-of-purchase product sales are acceptable within secondary schools?" and "Who decides?"

In 2007, Maine became the first state to outlaw brand-specific marketing of unhealthy foods during the school day. However, state law states excludes advertising on broadcast and in print media (e.g., newspapers and magazines), clothing with brand images worn on school grounds, or advertising on product packaging. A 2010 study of school compliance with the Maine legislation revealed that 45 percent of all marketing found was for products owned by either Coca-Cola or PepsiCo.

The noncompliant marketing on vending machines is mostly found in teacher's lounges, and the noncompliant posters are mostly found in athletic areas.[22] The study also found that administrators often do not know about the statewide ban and may also be confused by the difference between the ban in marketing and the nutrition standards for those products actually sold in schools. Educating educators about state and federal guidelines is essential in cultivating healthy teens and healthy schools.

Beyond food policy, there is much educators can learn by studying food. Marcus Weaver-Hightower writes in "Why Education Researchers Should Take School Food Seriously" that:

When school food is viewed as a bodily necessity, as distraction, solely as nutrition, or as a joke, there is little to recommend giving it serious consideration. I argue, however, that we can and should instead view food as an integral component of the ecology of education—the broader interconnections of actors, relationships, conditions, and processes of which education is composed.[23]

From this perspective, food can serve as both curricular and pedagogical lens. Educators also have the ability—even responsibility—to intentionally construct a school cafeteria environment that is conducive to healthy choices and behaviors.

The Smarter Lunchroom Movement from Dr. Brian Wansink, a researcher in consumer behavior and health marketing at Cornell University, attempts to instill better nutritional habits in children by "psyching kids out." Wansink calls attention to the ways in which the environment of lunchrooms shape young people's food choices. For example, the mere display of fruit in an attractive bowl in a well-lit spot in the school cafeteria lunch line increased sales of fruit by 104 percent. Sales also dramatically increased when bean burritos were embellished with the name "Big Bad Bean Burrito." Wansink also found that students were more likely to choose the first vegetable seen in a buffet line than the third vegetable. In this case, the cafeteria can serve as a classroom and food services as the curriculum—particularly for the thirty-two million students who participate in the National School Lunch and Breakfast programs.

The Politics of Healthy Schools

In June 2011 the Obama administration through the surgeon general released a National Prevention Strategy for prevention and wellness headed by seventeen agencies. The idea was to increase governmental funding for health in all federal, state, and local policies. The scope of "healthy environments," however, was limited to food, housing, transportation, community structures (including schools), and the natural environment. Noticeably absent was the accountability of corporations, particularly media corporations, and marketers within the health ecosystem.

The National Prevention Strategy instead framed media environments as an audience-centered responsibility and included it within a section titled "Empowered People." Also absent was responsibility or accountability of corporate producers and distributors:

> Mass media and social media can be used to help promote health and well-being. Individuals' decisions are influenced by how environments are designed and how choices are presented. Small changes to the environment in which people make decisions can support an individual's ability to make healthy choices. For example, making stairwells more attractive and safe increases their use and placing healthy options near cash registers can increase their likelihood of purchase.[24]

Increasing the attractiveness of stairwells and placing healthy options near cash registers may instigate small yet significant changes. Yet they are eclipsed by billions of marketing dollars of corporations such as McDonald's and Budweiser—two of the most-advertised brands in 2012.[25] When the primary identification of an individual is consumer of a "healthy" product, their voice and vote are limited to what money can buy. Policymaking that suggests individuals construct their own healthy media environments within the existing oppressive institutional structures is misleading and ultimately counterproductive.

Efforts at constructing a healthy school environment are hindered as public schools increasingly rely upon corporate advertising to fund field trips, uniforms, and technology that would otherwise go unfunded due to budget cuts. High school campuses are saturated with product marketing across textbooks, scoreboards, hallways, cafeterias, and even rooftops. In 2005, nearly half of all public elementary schools and about 80 percent of public high schools operated under exclusive "pouring rights" contracts where either Coca-Cola or Pepsi supplies all the beverages sold in school.[26] The contracts can include millions of dollars upfront with hundreds of thousands of dollars annually (not a large sum of money for school districts), and contracts can extend for a decade or longer. Opponents of pouring rights contracts point out the compulsory nature of public education relegates teenagers to a captive audience, continuously exposed at school to marketing messages for unhealthy products. Proponents of advertising in schools situate commercial advertising as a small price to pay for funding, equipment, and technology to which educators and students would otherwise not have access.

The social values circulated through popular culture and mass media are understandably part of the capitalistic, free-market economy of the United States. However, the ease of access of corporate culture to U.S. public schools and the inability or unwillingness of educational agencies to cordon off marketing practices that target youth between the ages of twelve and seventeen is a serious concern. When Michelle Obama travels to schools across the country emphasizing increased individual physical fitness with the inspirational mantra of "Let's Move," it does not diminish the responsibility of Congress to hold the food and beverage industries accountable for their manufacturing and marketing practices. In sum, the unquestioned acceptance of corporate practices within schools has far-reaching consequences for our teenagers, our communities, and public health in general.

MOVING FORWARD

Shortly after the Beyoncé Pepsi controversy, the *Let's Move!* campaign switched gears in a small yet significant way. Michelle Obama partnered with the WAT-AAH! bottled water company and the Partnership for Healthier America in the 2014 "Drink Up" campaign that encourages children to drink more water. The campaign emphasized the sugar-free properties of water—a subtle yet direct contradiction to the Pepsi marketing messages promoted through Beyoncé less than a year prior.

The same year that Beyoncé partnered with PepsiCo, the WAT-AAH! Foundation (in partnership with Fit Kids) conducted a focus group study of the impact and influence of celebrity-endorsed commercial advertisements on teenagers. The study revealed that teens consider celebrities to be role models, are inspired by their attributes, and are admittedly influenced to buy celebrity-endorsed products. However, the study also found that when teens are asked to reflect on 1) the motivations of food and beverage companies to use celebrities; 2) the celebrities' motivation for endorsing the products; and 3) the health effects of the products advertised, their purchase intent drops dramatically—from 77 percent to 23 percent.[27] The study essentially argued that media literacy education among teenagers can essentially counteract the messages of celebrity endorsements.

The WAT-AHH! study findings were a double-edged sword for Michelle Obama, who at first leveraged Beyoncé's celebrity power for *Let's Move!* but then diluted that same celebrity power through the WAT-AHH! study. Undoubtedly the WAT-AHH! bottled water company profited from the political partnership and research findings. Is it also worth questioning the extent to which the research findings are reputable, as they conveniently counteract the marketing tactics used by their competitors in the beverage industry. If nothing else, the WAT-AAH! study findings present an intriguing springboard for more systematic research on the power and potential of health literacy education within the media ecology of teenagers.

The *Let's Move!* Pepsi controversy is microcosmic of the larger popular culture of celebrity endorsement from which teenagers cannot escape. It is also subtle in its portrayal of the complex relationships among corporate capitalism, government policy, public health, and schooling in the United States. The impact of the *Let's Move!* campaign on twelve- to nineteen-year-olds is not yet established and questions abound with regards to its ultimate success without the support of policy structures or without changes within the food and beverage industries. The pendulum once again swings away from holding corporations and industries accountable toward bolstering individual responsibility for health.

NOTES

1. Peggy Edwards and Agis Tsouros, "Promoting Physical Activity and Active Living in Urban Environments: The Role of Local Governments," Copenhagen, Den-

mark: World Health Organization Europe, 2006. http://www.euro.who.int/__data/assets/pdf_file/0009/98424/E89498.pdf, ix.

2. "Let's Move! Learn the Facts," http://www.letsmove.gov/learn-facts/epidemic-childhood-obesity, 2010, §10.

3. Sabina B. Gesell, Eric Tesdahl, and Eileen Ruchman, "The Distribution of Physical Activity in an After-School Friendship Network," *Pediatrics* 129.6 (2012): 1064–71.

4. Kia Macarechi, "Obama Says 'Beyoncé Could Not Be a Better Role Model for My Girls' as Event with Jay-Z Nets $4 Million," *Huffington Post*, September 19, 2012, http://www.huffingtonpost.com/2012/09/19/obama-beyonce-role-model-jay-z-4-million_n_1896368.html. See also Lisa Respers France, "Michelle Obama and Beyoncé: BFFs," *CNN Entertainment*, January 17, 2014, http://www.cnn.com/2014/01/17/showbiz/celebrity-news-gossip/michelle-obama-beyonce-friendship/.

5. Grace Elizabeth Hale, "When Jim Crow Drank Coke," *New York Times*, January 28, 2013, http://www.nytimes.com/2013/01/29/opinion/when-jim-crow-drank-coke.html?_r=0.

6. Ashley P. Lowe and George Hacker, *Selfish Giving: How The Soda Industry Uses Philanthropy to Sweeten Its Profits*. Washington, DC: Center for Science in the Public Interest, 2013, ii.

7. Lowe and Hacker, *Selfish Giving*, 13.

8. PepsiCo is not alone in their marketing practices. Since 1986 Coca-Cola has donated at least US$2.1 million to the NAACP and has also awarded grants to the Hispanic Federation. Coca-Cola also launched "My Coke Rewards" in 2013 to target urban communities through the Sprite Spark Parks campaign. Consumer votes determine the twenty-five school grants to refurbish urban plan areas, which automatically includes the installation of a Sprite billboard.

9. See http://familydoctor.org/familydoctor/en/prevention-wellness/food-nutrition/nutrients/hydration-why-its-so-important.html, 6.

10. Lee Fang, "Where Have All the Lobbyists Gone? On Paper, the Influence-Peddling Business Is Drying Up. But Lobbying Money Is Flooding into Washington, DC, Like Never Before. What's Going On?" March 10, 2014, *The Nation*, http://www.thenation.com/article/178460/shadow-lobbying-complex.

11. Marion Nestle, "How Regulation Really Does Change Eating Behavior," September 4, 2012, *The Atlantic*, http://www.theatlantic.com/health/archive/2012/09/how-regulation-really-does-change-eating-behavior/261908/.

12. Lowe and Hacker, "Selfish Giving," 9.

13. "Nestle Urged Not to Market Girl Scouts Candy Bars to Kids," CSPI, June 18, 2012, http://www.cspinet.org/new/201206181.html.

14. Rob Moodie, David Stuckler, Carlos Monteiro, Nick Sheron, Bruce Neal, Thaksaphon Thamarangsi, Paul Lincoln, and Sally Casswell, "Profits and Pandemics: Prevention of Harmful Effects of Tobacco, Alcohol, and Ultra-Processed Food and Drink Industries," *Lancet* 381 (2013): 670–79.

15. Moodie et al., "Profits and Pandemics," 670.

16. Tom Philpott, "Is the Junk Food Industry Buying the WHO?" *Mother Jones*, November 1, 2012, http://www.motherjones.com/tom-philpott/2012/10/junk-food-industry-buys-influence-global-level-too.

17. Nestle, "How Regulation Really Does Change."

18. Rachel Dissell, "County Places Obese Cleveland Heights Child in Foster Care," *Cleveland.com*, November 26, 2011, http://blog.cleveland.com/metro/2011/11/obese_cleveland_heights_child.html.

19. Moodie et al., "Profits and Pandemics," 677.

20. Moodie et al., "Profits and Pandemics," 674.

21. Winnie Hu, "Schools Dangle Carrot Snacks, but It's a Tough Sale," *New York Times*, October 3, 2011, http://www.nytimes.com/2011/10/04/education/04vending.html?pagewanted=all&_r=0.

22. Michele Polacsek, Karen O'Rourke, Liam O'Brien, Janet Whatley Blum, and Sara Donahue, "Examining Compliance with a Statewide Law Banning Junk Food and

Beverage Marketing in Maine Schools," *Public Health Reports* 127, (2012 Mar-Apr) no. 2: 216–23.

23. Marcus B. Weaver-Hightower, "Why Education Researchers Should Take School Food Seriously," *Educational Researcher* 40, no. 1 (2011): 16, doi: 10.3102/0013189X10397043.

24. National Prevention Council, "Strategic Directions: Empowered People," *National Prevention Strategy: America's Plan for Better Health and Wellness*. Washington, DC: U.S. Department of Health and Human Services, Office of the Surgeon General, June 2011, 24.

25. "Infographic: Meet America's 25 Biggest Advertisers," *Advertising Age*, July 8, 2013, http://adage.com/article/news/meet-america-s-25-biggest-advertisers/242969/.

26. Tom Philpott, "80 Percent of Public Schools Have Contracts with Coke or Pepsi," *Mother Jones*, August 15, 2012, http://www.motherjones.com/tom-philpott/2012/08/schools-limit-campus-junk-food-have-lower-obesity-rates.

27. "Understanding the Impact of Celebrities in Food & Beverage Advertising." New York: The WAT-AAH! Foundation, 2013.

FIVE

A Healthy Curriculum

Jamie Oliver's Food Revolution aired on U.S. television between March 2010 and June 2011. Its star was English celebrity chef and restaurateur Jamie Oliver, and the show documented Oliver's attempt to help Americans fight obesity. Oliver's mantra was "start a revolution with real people and real change." The first episode takes place in Huntington, West Virginia, one of the unhealthiest towns in the United States. The show documents Oliver trying to improve the eating habits of the residents—but not without opposition.

In the second season, Oliver visits Los Angeles, California, on a mission to change school meals. Oliver clashes with cafeteria staff over the pizza served for breakfast and the chicken nuggets and flavored milk for lunch. The show depicts the difficulty in introducing change within one of the largest school systems in the United States. Despite the show winning an Emmy Award in 2010, it was cancelled in 2011, and Oliver was ultimately barred from filming at any Los Angeles public school. The audience is reminded that the daily schedule, student motivation, and the bureaucracies of the school system cannot be separated from the wider social, political, and economic contexts in which they exist. In other words, schools are complicated organisms.[1]

In the early 1900s, educational reformer John Dewey promoted, among other things, experiential education where children learned by doing, exercising their bodies and their minds and learning outside the classroom to explore nature.[2] For Dewey, the role of the teacher was that of a facilitator or guide for student-led inquiry. A century later, research in the area of embodied cognition finds that our bodily experiences can shape the way we think.[3] In other words, students who physically step out of the classroom are more creative and think outside the box. Perhaps the most obvious pathway to health literacy education is to literally and figuratively step outside the classroom.

Dewey's philosophy of education clashed with the twentieth-century efficiency-oriented model of schooling that focused more on academics and didactic instruction. The efficiency model of schooling continues in the present day where teachers feel pressured to "cover" as much content as possible and teach to the test. In an era of teacher evaluation based on student standardized test scores and growth objectives (SGOs), experiential or project-based learning is considered radical and even disruptive. This chapter moves the standards-based approach to integrating health literacy and curriculum, toward a transdisciplinary model that engages students beyond the classroom.

A STANDARDS-BASED APPROACH

Like rapid technological change, health education is a moving target. The basic hygiene curriculum in schools in the late nineteenth century aimed to reduce the risk of contracting communicable diseases like tuberculosis. In the early twentieth century, the focus of health education was on temperance or alcohol education. In the 1920s, sex education was promoted to counter the effect of sexuality portrayed in movies. By the end of the twentieth century the high school health curriculum included hygiene, nutrition, sexuality, drugs, traffic safety, accident prevention, physical activity, AIDS/HIV prevention, and mental health.[4]

In the twenty-first century, new health-related topics have emerged, including cyber safety; anti-harassment, intimidation, and bullying; and distracted driving, among others—all to be addressed under the ever-expanding umbrella of health education.[5] Since public health in the United States is historically grounded in the reduction of mortality and morbidity from disease, it is not surprising to find that health education in schools has traditionally been problem-based and focused on avoidance of health risk behaviors rather than promotion of positive health behaviors.[6]

Link to Academic Achievement

The turn of the twenty-first century brought with it recognition of the link between good health and educational achievement. Research links health to increased student attentiveness, less classroom disruption, higher self-esteem, less depression, and less anxiety.[7] Numerous studies also show significant positive relationships between physical fitness and academic achievement, including improved performance on standardized tests.[8]

Although physical activity is not the only determining factor of adolescent health, many doctors agree that it plays a central role.[9] Students with higher grades are less likely to be physically inactive and engage in unhealthy dietary behaviors than their classmates with lower grades. Students who are physically active and do not engage in unhealthy dietary behaviors receive higher grades than their classmates who are physically inactive and engage in unhealthy dietary behaviors.[10] There is a *correlation* between health and education; however, it is difficult to establish a clear *causal* relationship between health and academic achievement.[11, 12] School administrators are therefore faced with a deficit model where poor health inhibits learning but that good health doesn't necessarily lead to academic achievement.[13]

At present only five states (Illinois, Iowa, Massachusetts, New Mexico, and Vermont) require physical education across grades K–12, and only two states (New Jersey and Rhode Island) require it across grades 1–12.[14] A mere 8 percent of middle schools and 2 percent of high schools in the United States provide the nationally recommended daily physical education or its equivalent for the entire school year for students in all grades in the school.[15] And while the Centers for Disease Control (CDC) reports that 84 percent of middle schools and 95 percent of high schools *require* physical education, the vast majority of students do not receive the nationally recommended *amount* of physical education.[16, 17]

The current U.S. guidelines recommend that teens engage in an hour or more of moderate-intensity to vigorous aerobic physical activity each day. This can include brisk walking, jogging, or swimming—in at least ten-minute bouts. Research also indicates that "lifestyle activities" such as walking to and from school have a more lasting effect than regimented activities such as calisthenics or jogging.[18] Longitudinal research finds that exercise during youth impacts cognitive health later on in life. In the longitudinal UK National Child Development Study, researchers examined levels of exercise of more than nine thousand participants over time, beginning in 1958. Data were collected at the age of eleven, sixteen, thirty-three, forty-two, forty-six, and fifty. The study found that those who exercised weekly as a child and as an adult performed better on tests of memory, learning, attention, and reasoning at the age of fifty than those who exercised two or three times per month or less.[19]

Educators are aware of the benefits of physical education, yet time allotted for physical activity has severely declined over the past decade. Principals cite budget cuts, an increasing focus on standardized test preparation, and in some cases simply a lack of space or facilities.[20]

When it comes to promoting physical activity in schools, a meta-analysis of the research shows that curriculum strategies used in isolation are not effective.[21] Furthermore, adding physical education to classroom curriculum does not bring about substantial increases in physical activity, and there is a lack of evidence that physical education within school increases physical activity outside of school.[22]

The current national agenda (Healthy People 2020) differs from previous years in its expansion to include health-enhancing social and physical environments across the lifespan.[23] The forty-year-old model of health education (as an academic subject with teachers and students convening for five class periods a week for at least one semester in middle and senior high school levels) must adapt to meet the evolving needs of adolescent students. The twenty-first century is a time when increasing student health knowledge through the dissemination of information is inadequate education.[24] The task therefore as educators is to catalyze health literacy *skills* into positive health *behaviors* among teenagers. In other words, we must focus less on the deficit of health *illiteracy* among teenagers and hone the advantages of health literacy *practices*.

A Mandate to Integrate

In 2002, tech businessman Ken Kay cofounded the Partnership for 21st Century Skills "to serve as a catalyst to position 21st century readiness at the center of US K12 education by building collaborative partnerships among education, business, community and government leaders."[25] Founding organizations included AOL Time Warner, Apple Computer, and Microsoft, among others. The P21 Framework identifies health literacy as one of several interdisciplinary themes that should be woven throughout core subjects: Global Awareness; Financial, Economic, Business, and Entrepreneurial Literacy; Civic Literacy; Health Literacy; and Environmental Literacy. In 2004 the National Institute of Medicine followed a similar vein with *Health Literacy: A Prescription to End Confusion* that set forth recommendations to incorporate health-related tasks, materials, and examples into existing reading, writing, and mathematics lesson plans.[26]

In 2010 the U.S. Department of Health and Human Services through *A National Action Plan to Improve Health Literacy* identified health literacy education as a priority area. The plan specifically identified the type of education where "students can learn to be critical thinkers and seekers of health information.[27] The 2010 *National Action Plan* also set forth the goal that all preservice teachers have coursework in the instructional methods of health education; that all practicing teachers engage in professional development of health education teaching strategies and skills; and that teachers embed health-related tasks, skills, and examples into existing K–12 science, math, literacy, social studies, and computer instruction.[28]

An example of an integrative approach is Chicago-based Healthy Schools Campaign, founded in 2002 for the purpose of creating equitable access to healthier school environments, particularly for low-income and minority children. Their approach is holistic and comprehensive:

Wellness is not relegated to an occasional health lesson or physical education class—it is part of math, science, lunch and everything in between. It means providing teachers with professional development related to children's physical and emotional development, and integrating health into every subject, reward system and classroom management strategy. In this environment, good nutrition, physical activity, basic safety, clean air and water, access to care and education about how to make healthy choices allow students to thrive. [29]

An integrated approach is also found in Planet Health, an inquiry-based curriculum produced by educators and scientists at the Harvard School of Public Health. [30] The curriculum is designed for teachers across all subject areas and aligned with the Massachusetts Department of Education Curriculum Frameworks (learning standards) for health, language arts, math, science and technology, and history and social science. The curriculum asks middle school students to think holistically about the interrelatedness of health behaviors and engages students in active discussions to encourage higher-level thinking and cognition.

For example, in one of the "Balanced Diet" thematic lessons ("Problem-Solving: Making Healthy Choices"), students are asked, in part, to apply mathematical thinking and calculations to make healthier menu choices at a fast-food restaurant. This activity requires students to interpret information, plan a problem-solving strategy, draw conclusions, and defend their conclusions:

> You are at the mall with a group of friends. You promised your mom that you would buy a nutritious meal with the $6 she gave you to spend on dinner. McDonald's, Domino's Pizza, and Subway are your favorite restaurants. Is it possible to buy a meal at one of these fast-food restaurants that is well balanced (focusing on grains, fruits, and vegetables) and contains only a moderate amount of fat and minimizes the intake of unhealthy fat? Assume you've already eaten two-thirds of the recommended servings for fruits and vegetables in the meals and snack that you had today, and you have consumed two-thirds of the recommended daily total fat and saturated fat intake. Look at the healthy eating guidelines and the fast-food menus on the student resource sheets. Plan a meal that helps you meet the minimum requirements for fruits and vegetables and that does not exceed the recommended daily grams of total fat and saturated fat. Be prepared to defend your choices. [31]

Another Planet Health lesson ("Passing the Sugar") integrates chemistry, physiology, math, and health concepts. Students estimate the number of sodas and sport drinks they drink in a week and calculate and measure out the grams and teaspoons of sugar contained in these drinks. They are also introduced to the chemical structure and function of simple sugars and learn how the digestive, cardiorespiratory, and endocrine systems interact to deliver fuel to muscles. Students are also asked to investigate the sugar content of foods found in their homes.[32]

Enacting health literacy education according to an interdisciplinary model is analogous to the interconnections that comprise the World Wide Web. There are seemingly infinite connections between and across disciplines. The nodes that connect math with nutrition, science, anatomy, chemistry, cooking, and English create new knowledge across and between these disciplines. An integrated approach to health literacy can improve students' learning across several content areas and therefore has the potential to contribute to higher test scores on states' subject area standardized tests.[33] However, state policies that link standardized test scores with student promotion and graduation tend to undermine the implementation of health and media literacies across the curriculum.

In recent years, the focus on adolescent learning has shifted to cross-disciplinary efforts to increase school connectedness, the belief by students that adults in the school care about their learning as well as about them as individuals. [34] Recent research suggests that next to the influence of family, school connectedness is the second most influential protective factor against emotional distress, disordered eating, and suicide.[35, 36, 37] School connectedness is also correlated with higher attendance, higher grades, and higher test scores.[38] A means of increasing school connectedness among adolescents is to ensure relevancy and authenticity of curriculum.

Relevancy is found in the curriculum of FoodFight, a New York City nonprofit started by two high school teachers, Carolyn Cohen and Deborah Lewison-Grant. The teachers created FoodFight in response to the obesity crisis they witnessed firsthand with students in their own classrooms. The teachers developed a three-part food literacy curriculum for high school students that focuses on food advertising, nutrition, and social advocacy. The program brings scientists and gardeners into the school classroom to work with high school students, their parents, teachers, and school staff. As a result of their in-school curriculum, they have seen changes in out-of-school health-related behaviors:

> After a lesson about the consequences of consuming too much sugar, Ms. Newton switched from McDonald's sweetened iced tea to a no-calorie drink, Ms. Tonda said, and now brings bottled water to class. Another student, affected by the images of a crowded chicken farm in the documentary "Food Inc.," has asked her mother to stop buying meat from industrial producers.[39]

These interdisciplinary connections can yield higher-level knowledge and skills. However, it may not necessarily provide a holistic perspective that is needed to guide behavior. For example, John Evans and Emma Rich collected life stories from young women experiencing eating disorders and found that the dominant narrative of obesity in the context of adolescent education and curriculum was subversive rather than condu-cive to the enactment of healthy behaviors.[40] These and other researchers argue that despite formal health literacy education, a large number of adolescents still engage in unhealthy behaviors and that schools need health-promoting media literacy education beyond the school class-room.[41]

A TRANSDISCIPLINARY APPROACH

A transdisciplinary approach to curriculum is holistic and interconnects all subject area disciplines into a coherent whole. A transdisciplinary approach affords multiple layers of meaning and complexity. The goal is for students to understand health as an ecosystem and then systematical-ly act on that knowledge based on a systemic understanding. Curriculum must therefore move beyond the cognitive level and address social fac-tors, attitudes, values, norms, and skills that influence specific health-related behaviors.[42]

An ecological perspective on human development deepens under-standing of individual agency and how it interacts across multilayered and interacting contexts.[43] It acknowledges the constellation of factors involved in teen health behaviors, including (but not limited) to an indi-vidual's characteristics, home life, school, work, community interactions, social networks, government, and media habits. Learning transcends the school curriculum and plays out in the wider life context of the student, as the following two examples illustrate.

Lessons from NeverSeconds

In April 2012, nine-year-old Martha Payne with the help of her father started her own blog (neverseconds.blogspot.com) as part of a school writing project at Lochgilphead Primary School in Argyll, Scotland. She decided to combine her school assignment with her general disappoint-ment with the quality and quantity of food comprising her school lunches. Her goal was to hone her writing skills and to raise a few dollars for her favorite charity, Mary's Meals, that coordinates school feeding projects in communities around the world.

In the process, Payne captured less-than-flattering photos of her school lunch tray and wrote meticulously descriptive commentary that rated each meal with a "food-o-meter" and counted the number of bites required to consume it (the meals on average scored 7 out of 10). In at least one instance, Payne complained that it was not enough food to help her focus on her schoolwork—inspiring her blog title, "NeverSeconds," after the school policy against second portions.

After a local paper published an unflattering story in reaction to Payne's blog (implying the lunch workers should be fired), the local school council reacted by banning Payne from further publishing photos of her school lunches on her blog. Bewildered by the controversy, Payne stated she was upset at having to stop her writing project halfway through the process.[44] Martha then started posting pictures of school lunches sent to her by children in Germany, Japan, Spain, Taiwan, and the United States. The banning of posting school lunch photos prompted a global outcry through social media and a public relations nightmare for the local school council.

By June 2012 Payne's blog had surpassed three million hits. Under much public (even worldwide) pressure, the council then lifted the ban. The powerful images of her school lunches resonated throughout the world, and compelled responses from other high profile food celebrities who championed her cause via Twitter. Soon after the ban was lifted, it was announced that Martha would be teaming up with a celebrity chef to help the council provide more nutritious meals at her school.[45] With her emergent fame, Payne's NeverSeconds blog page views surpassed five million hits. While Payne's original goal was to raise £10,000 for charity, she ultimately raised more than £100,000, enough to feed thousands of schoolchildren in Malawi for more than a year.

In June 2012 Payne traveled to Malawi to see the two thousand children fed by the kitchen constructed by "Mary's Meals" and named by Payne as "Friends of NeverSeconds." With the help of her father, Martha co-wrote a book about her experience—with the proceeds of each book sold to go toward feeding twenty-five children in Malawi.

Payne's story illustrates the profound social, political, and economic impact of a school writing assignment and the power of social media to propel learning well beyond the bounds of the school classroom and even to a global level. The civic engagement piece of this story is even more profound. Payne serendipitously mobilized a worldwide community to not only initiate change in her local school culture but also to enact change on a global scale by leveraging donations and diverting them to feed schoolchildren in Malawi.

Students from around the word engaged as contributing authors to Payne's blog, sharing images of their own school lunches. Harshi from India posts on Neverseconds:

> Today my lunch includes multi grains. Pesarattu—It is a dosa made with whole green grams. And it was spicy. It has a high protein content. You can call them green gram pancakes. I had them with yoghurt. Then I had some stir fried beans and beets. They are spiced up with pepper. I love vegetables! Usually I have to stay in school for after-school sports which for me is table tennis. So I need something to eat for the evenings. So I got a vegetable spring roll and a multi grain cupcake. My mom made the cake with flour which contains 4 or more

grains, Raisins and cashews. In India we call the flour "Saththu mavu" which means nutritive flour. The grains are Ragi, Maize, Wheat, Bajra. This flour is mixed with usual cake flour to make the cake. It was not as soft as the cake made with white flour. But it tastes just as good. Usually while eating me and my friends share our food.[46]

Payne's singular voice provided an opportunity for many others to be educated—and not just about (un)healthy school lunches. There are lessons here about civil dissent, school policy, equity, global citizenship, and social justice. There are threads of language arts, critical thinking, argumentation and debate, health literacy, and politics that comprise a rich tapestry of curriculum.

The significance of Payne's father throughout this story cannot be understated—from helping her initially set up her blog to navigating the controversy and helping his daughter manage the media attention, even co-participating in press interviews. It is significant that Payne's father insists they "never wanted to campaign."[47] In a radio interview, he explains, "It was a writing project. She's interested in becoming a journalist and my goodness, she's had something of a lesson in how modern day journalism can go viral."[48] Under the guidance of her father, Payne is learning important lessons about the moral values of care, compassion, civility, charity, and civic-mindedness.

Although Payne's blog was part of a formal school assignment, ultimately it was guided by the motives of Payne, her father, and eventually a crowdsourced online community. The uses of social media were like the ground shifting from underneath her as she navigated the unexpected controversy and the exacerbated consequences in real time and in public for the world to see. Accompanied by her father, Payne herself stated in an interview "It's quite annoying all the people that want to talk to me." The construct of health was flipped—away from an internal state of being to a social and political goal that involved social change and helping others.

Lessons from the Edible Schoolyard

In 1971 chef Alice Waters founded Chez Panisse restaurant in Berkeley, California, with the philosophy that "cooking should be based on the finest and freshest seasonal ingredients that are produced sustainably and locally."[49] Over the course of four decades, Waters has emerged as a culinary expert, author, pioneer for local farming, proponent of sustainable agriculture, and a strong advocate for public education. In 1996 after noticing an asphalt-covered, open plot of land in the yard of Martin Luther King, Jr. Middle School near her restaurant, Waters commented in a local newspaper that the school she passed every day "looked like no one cared about it."[50]

The principal of the school reached out to Waters and collaboration began among teachers, families, and the local community. Over the course of several years, Waters worked with parent volunteers and the community to transform more than an acre of asphalt into a school garden, called the Edible Schoolyard (ESY). Waters notes, "It took several years of cover crop to get some of the poisons out of the ground."[51] The meticulous efforts were built on Waters's belief that when children are involved in the growing and preparing of food, they want to eat it, ultimately providing a long-term solution for the ongoing health crisis. After recruiting the Center for Ecoliteracy as another collaborator (and funder) Waters was able to hire a full-time garden director. The ESY continued to expand as students cleared trees and brush to place two 3,500-gallon cisterns to collect the rainwater for irrigation. They also built a chicken coop for an expanding flock of chickens and ducks.

By the third year of its inception, the ESY expanded to include a teaching kitchen. Teachers, parents, and community members came together to transform an abandoned school cafeteria into the kitchen classroom.[52] The garden and kitchen directors worked with teachers to generate lessons linked to classroom studies—such as teaching fractions in the kitchen by measuring ingredients and teaching about early civilizations by growing heirloom grains. Measuring the garden beds and counting seeds were also part and parcel of the math curriculum. Students participate in all aspects of growing, harvesting, and preparing garden-grown food during the school day and in after-school classes. They learn to think critically and more deeply about the food they eat. Students learn about civilizations, including the history of food and the plight of the farmer.

The goal was to change the relationship between children and food while simultaneously creating interactive experiences to interconnect history, math, and science. By the fifth year and with a staff of eight people, ESY taught ten ninety-minute classes a week in both the garden and the kitchen. The staff was also able to expand the relationship with the broader school community by hosting traditional school celebrations such as Family Writing Night and the English Language Learners Dinner. The annual Mother's Day Plant Sale has become a significant community and fund-raising event. The ESY Project has also integrated itself into the standards-based educational culture:

> At ESY Berkeley, we have designed our curriculum of 62 lessons for middle school students to meet a specific set of edible education learning goals (which we refer to as ESY standards). At the same time, these lessons support California subject area standards and are aligned to the Common Core State Standards. The goal of the ESY curriculum is to empower students with the knowledge and values to make food choices that are healthy for them, their communities, and the environment.[53]

Eighth graders learn the six essential elements of life (carbon, hydrogen, nitrogen, oxygen, phosphorus, and sulfur) and how they function in the garden. They build, tend, and sift a compost pile and then explain how fungus, bacteria, and invertebrates are part of decomposition. Students prepare soft pretzels, which requires them to activate yeast and observe the production of carbon dioxide.[54]

By 2013 there were 551 school gardens worldwide, 279 academic classrooms, and 241 kitchen classrooms that have adopted the ESY model. These include schools in Australia, Italy, Canada, Great Britain, and Ecuador. Each year the ESY team hosts thousands of people on public tours. For the past four years a small number of educators from around the world have completed an intensive summer teaching academy to learn how to begin edible education programs in their own communities. The goal is to continue developing hands-on outreach and eventually bring ESY institutes to member locations.[55]

In 2003, Waters's foundation launched the School Lunch Initiative in an effort to transform school lunches. Ultimately, Waters was able to create a sustainable organic garden and landscape that is wholly integrated into the school's curriculum, culture, and food program. The school itself is simply the institutional vehicle for a larger social and cultural shift that must take place. Many of the challenges of scaling up what is now called the "Edible Education" movement have to do with school budget cuts and a shrunken school curriculum due to standardized tests. Other schools within Berkeley Unified School District also vie for the same funds as Waters's high-profile program in MLK Middle School. Waters says scaling up requires federal and state funds that are dedicated to edible education.

For Waters and ESY, good health is the right of every child and health literacy is an essential goal of education. As such, edible education should play a major role in schooling in the United States. Through hands-on experiential learning and the curricular integration of garden, classroom, and cafeteria, students learn to critically think about their food and local and world cultures, and in turn develop a mindful, respectful relationship to food. The use of online video conveys the aesthetic and naturalistic power of the ESY to a global audience, and the online social network cultivates unity as a mechanism for transforming the school lunch-as-curriculum.

The value of adult leadership and role modeling as scaffolding for students cannot be understated. In the ESY, Waters entered as a culinary pioneer and passionate advocate for sustainable agriculture. She was already a veteran practitioner of an "eco-gastronomic" curriculum, making her entry into formal schooling a natural step in furthering her agenda to "teach, nurture and empower young people" and make a humane and sustainable future accessible to all children.[56] Although Waters does not directly interface with students as a classroom teacher, her expertise, leadership, and example were paramount to the initial success of ESY and the outgrowth of collateral programs. Questions that emerge include, "What leadership qualities and structures are essential to cultivating health among young people?" and "What role can apprenticeships play in health literacy education?"

Nearly a century has passed since the establishment of high schools in the United States and we continue to struggle with the role of schools in addressing health education. The U.S. Department of Health and Human Services asserts that school programs can promote physical activity and healthy eating, reduce the rate of overweight and obesity among teenagers, and improve academic achievement.[57] This is a tall order for schools that are increasingly cash strapped, administratively burdened with standardized testing, experience high teacher attrition, and are charged with closing the achievement gap.

A transdisciplinary approach to health literacy requires each individual to take personal responsibility for health and to see health as a cognitive, social, and political activity.[58] From this perspective, health is both a democratic right and a civic responsibility—to change those structures for the purpose of the common good of public health. It follows that educators and administrators as a collective scaffold student learning and civic engagement rather than simply focus on the individual's cognitive ability to analyze health messages.

A WHOLE SCHOOL MODEL

In 1968 Dr. James Comer, a Yale University child psychologist, developed the Comer Process, also known as the School Development Program. The Comer Process took a supportive view of education that focused on developing the "whole" child, including paying attention to academic growth, emotional wellness, social and moral development, and a collaborative school approach to learning. A Comer school resembles a community center and emphasizes the link between school and social services. The Comer method has improved achievement in high poverty and high minority urban settings. It is self-described as "not a project or add-on, but rather an operating system—a way of managing, organizing, coordinating, and integrating programs and activities."[59] A Comer school places collective responsibility on principals, administrators, teachers, and parents to make collaborative decisions that are in the best interest of the student.

In the 1980s a similar systemic approach to health education emerged in Europe and North America. Rather than looking at individual health problems, a comprehensive or Coordinated School Health Program (CSHP) examined school health policies, the social and physical environment, school-based health services, and community partnerships. Using similar principles found in Comer's School Development Program, Coordinated School Health integrated school policies, physical environment, social environment, individual health skills and action competencies, community links, and health services.[60]

While most of the United States recognize the role of schools in promoting health, there is less agreement on how integrated it should be across the curriculum and whether it should include a health services component.[61] The challenge lies in potential misalignment between curricula and prevention services. For example, "health curricula in nearly two-thirds of states include the topics of HIV, sexually transmitted infections, and pregnancy. Yet, only one-fifth of states require schools to provide any preventative services related to these topics."[62]

It is up to state school wellness teams to coordinate the various programmatic and curricular opportunities for health education and community partnerships. These wellness teams consists of key stakeholders including administrators, principals, health and physical education teachers, as well as teachers in the core academic subjects, school nurse, food staff, maintenance staff, parents, students, PTA/PTO representative, and community members. Along similar lines, the Association for Supervision and Curriculum Development (ASCD) in 2007 established the Whole Child Initiative, which essentially reiterated the whole school model and privileged health, intellectually challenging yet "well-balanced" curriculum, safety, community engagement, and supportive leaders.

In July 2014, the CDC in partnership with the ASCD announced the "Whole School, Whole Community, Whole Child" model to more forcefully coordinate across school elements—such as incorporating exercise into after-school activities, revisiting cafeteria menu offerings, and increasing parental engagement. The model builds on the traditional coordinated school health approach and the whole child framework. The emphasis is on the relationship between learning and health and fosters collaboration between schools and communities. While this integrative approach makes sense, it remains to be seen the extent to which it will impact school policy and funding decisions.

NOTES

1. Ursula M. Franklin, *The Real World of Technology* (CBC Massey Lectures series), rev. ed. Ontario, Canada: House of Anansi Press, 1999, 154.

2. Sarah Mondale and Sarah B. Patton, eds., *School: The Story of American Public Education*. Boston: Beacon Press, 2001, 77.

3. Angela K.-y Leung, Suntae Kim, Evan Polman, Lay See Ong, Lin Qiu, Jack A. Goncalo, and Jeffrey Sanchez-Burks, "Embodied Metaphors and Creative 'Acts,'" *Psychological Science* 23, no. 5 (2012): 502–9, doi: 10.1177/0956797611429801.

4. Lawrence St. Leger, "What's the Place of Schools in Promoting Health? Are We Too Optimistic?" *Health Promotion International* 19, no. 4 (2004): 405–8, doi: 10.1093/heapro/dah401.

5. Currently a majority of U.S. schools are required by state-adopted policy to follow either the National Health Education Standards (NHES) or state health education standards. Although the NHES and the American Association of Health Education acknowledge health literacy as the intended outcome of the standards, they specify adoption and maintenance of healthy *behaviors* as the goal of school health education.

6. Tami Benham-Deal and Bonni Hodges, *Role of 21st Century Schools in Promoting Health Literacy*. Washington, DC: National Education Association Health Information Network, 2009.

7. Patti Neighmond, "Exercise Helps Students in the Classroom," National Public Radio, August 31, 2006, http://www.npr.org/templates/story/story.php?storyId=5742152.

8. See California Department of Education. *A Study of the Relationship between Physical Fitness and Academic Achievement in California Using 2004 Test Results*. Sacramento, CA: Department of Education, 2005. See also Texas Education Agency, "Physically Fit Students More Likely to Do Well in School, Less Likely to Be Discipline Problems." Austin: Texas Education Agency, 2009; U.S. Centers for Disease Control and Prevention, "The Association between School-Based Physical Activity, Including Physical Education, and Academic Performance." Atlanta, GA: U.S. Department of Health and Human Services, 2010.

9. T. Lobstein, L. Baur, and R. Uauy, "Obesity in Children and Young People: A Crisis in Public Health," *Obesity Review* 5 (2004): 4–85. See also K. S. Steinbeck, "The Importance of Physical Activity in the Prevention of Overweight and Obesity in Childhood: A Review and an Opinion," *Obesity Review* 2 (2001): 117–30.

10. "Physical Inactivity and Unhealthy Dietary Behaviors and Academic Achievement" [fact sheet], U.S. Department of Health and Human Services Center for Disease Control and Prevention. http://www.cdc.gov/HealthyYouth/health_and_academics. Accessed January 23, 2013.

11. Marion Nestle, *Food Politics: How the Food Industry Influences Nutrition and Health*. Berkeley: University of California Press, 2007, 401–5.

12. Peter Muennig, "How Education Produces Health: A Hypothetical Framework," *Teachers College Record*, September 12, 2007, http://www.tcrecord.org/content.asp?contentid=1460.

13. Barbara Devaney, Peter Schochet, Craig Thornton, Nancy Fasciang, and Amelia Gavin, *Evaluating the Effects of School Health Interventions on School Performance: Design Report*. Princeton, NJ: Mathematics Policy Research, Inc., 1993. See also World Bank, *World Development Report 1993*. New York: Oxford University Press, 1993.

14. Institute of Medicine (IOM), *Accelerating Progress in Obesity Prevention: Solving the Weight of the Nation*. Washington, DC: National Academies Press, 2012, 337.

15. U.S. Centers for Disease Control and Prevention, "SHPPS: School Health Policies and Practices Study," 2006, http://www.cdc.gov/HealthyYouth/shpps/.

16. U.S. Centers for Disease Control and Prevention, "SHPPS."

17. The U.S. surgeon general recommends that secondary schools require daily physical education in the amount of 225 minutes per week.

18. Oded Bar-Or and Tom Baranowski, "Physical Activity, Adiposity, and Obesity among Adolescents," *Pediatric Exercise Science* 6, no. 4 (1994): 348–60.

19. National Children's Bureau, "National Child Development Study Update 2014." http://www.cls.ioe.ac.uk/library-media/documents/NCDS_Leaflet_WEB.pdf.

20. Al Baker, "Despite Obesity Concerns, Gym Classes Are Cut." *New York Times*, July 10, 2012, http://www.nytimes.com/2012/07/11/education/even-as-schools-battle-obesity-physical-education-is-sidelined.html.

21. J. Salmon, Michael L. Booth, Philayrath Phongsavan, Niamh Murphy, and Anna Timperio, "Promoting Physical Activity Participation among Children and Adolescents," *Epidemiologic Reviews* 29 (2007), doi: 10.1093/epirev/mxm010. p. 146.

22. Salmon et al., "Promoting Physical Activity Participation among Children and Adolescents," 147.

23. U.S. Department of Health and Human Services, Office of Disease Prevention and Health Promotion, "Healthy People 2020 Framework," http://www.healthypeople.gov/sites/default/files/HP2020Framework.pdf.

24. Centers for Disease Control, "Characteristics of an Effective Health Education Curriculum," School Health Education Resources (SHER)," 2013, http://www.cdc.gov/Healthyyouth/SHER/characteristics/index.htm.

25. Partnership for 21st Century Skills, "Our Mission," http://www.p21.org/about-us/our-mission.

26. Lynn Nielsen-Bohlman, Allison M. Panzer, and David A. Kindig, eds., *Health Literacy: A Prescription to End Confusion*. Washington, DC: National Academies Press, 2004, 15.

27. U.S. Department of Health and Human Services, Office of Disease Prevention and Health Promotion, *National Action Plan to Improve Health Literacy*. Washington, DC, 2010, 33.

28. U.S. Department of Health and Human Services, *National Action Plan*, 34.

29. Healthy Schools Campaign, "Health in Mind: Integrating Health and Education," http://www.healthyschoolscampaign.org/programs/health-in-mind/.

30. Jill Carter, Jean Wiecha, Karen Peterson, Suzanne Nobrega, and Steven L. Gortmaker, *Planet Health: An Interdisciplinary Curriculum for Teaching Middle School Nutrition and Physical Activity*, 2nd ed. Champaign, IL: Human Kinetics, 2007.

31. Carter et al., *Planet Health*, 158.

32. Carter et al., *Planet Health*, 243–58.

33. Camille Martina, David Hursh, and Dina Markowitz, "Contradictions in Educational Policy: Implementing Integrated Problem-Based Environmental Health Curriculum in a High Stakes Environment," *Environmental Education Research* 15, no. 3 (2009): 279–97.

34. Adena M. Klem and James P. Connell, "Relationships Matter: Linking Teacher Support to Student Engagement and Achievement," *Journal of School Health* 74, no. 7 (2004): 262–73.

35. Michael D. Resnick, P. S. Bearman, and Robert William Blum, "Protecting Adolescents from Harm. Findings from the National Longitudinal Study on Adolescent Health," *Journal of the American Medical Association* 278, no. 10 (1997): 823–32.

36. Robert William Blum, Clea McNeely, and Peggy Mann Rinehart, *Improving the Odds: The Untapped Power of Schools to Improve the Health of Teens*. Minneapolis: Center for Adolescent Health and Development, University of Minnesota, 2002.

37. Michael D. Resnick, L. J. Harris, and Robert William Blum, "The Impact of Caring and Connectedness on Adolescent Health and Well-being," *Journal of Paediatrics & Child Health* 29 (suppl 1) (1993): S3–9.

38. Centers for Disease Control and Prevention, *School Connectedness: Strategies for Increasing Protective Factors among Youth*. Atlanta, GA: U.S. Department of Health and Human Services, 2009, 3.

39. Hannah Wallace, "In High Schools, a Critical Lens on Food," *New York Times*, October 26, 2011, A26.

40. Emma Rich, and John Evans, "'Fat Ethics'—The Obesity Discourse and Body Politics," *Social Theory and Health* 3 (2005): 341–58, doi: 10.1057/palgrave.sth.8700057.

41. Lynda Bergsma, "Media Literacy and Health Promotion for Adolescents," *Journal of Media Literacy Education* 3 (2011): 25.

42. Centers for Disease Control and Prevention, "Characteristics of an Effective Health Education Curriculum," February 27, 2013, http://www.cdc.gov/Healthyyouth/SHER/characteristics/index.htm.

43. Urie Bronfenbrenner, *The Ecology of Human Development*. Cambridge, MA: Harvard University Press, 1979. See also Urie Bronfenbrenner, "Ecology of the Family as a Context for Human Development: Research Perspectives," *Developmental Psychology* 22 (1986): 723–42.

44. Sarah Rainey, Alastair Good, and Richard Alleyne, "School Dinner Blogger Martha Payne Explains It Has Led to 'Big Improvements' in the Meals," *The Telegraph*,

June 22, 2012, http://www.telegraph.co.uk/news/uknews/9349845/School-dinner-blogger-Martha-Payne-explains-it-has-led-to-big-improvements-in-the-meals.html.

45. Scott Stump, "9-Year-Old Food Blogger to Overhaul School Lunches with Celeb Chef," Bites on *Today*, June 12, 2012, http://bites.today.com/_news/2012/06/18/12280863-9-year-old-food-blogger-to-overhaul-school-lunches-with-celeb-chef?lite.

46. "Goodbye and Thanks from Harshi," NeverSeconds: One Primary School Pupil's Daily Dose of School Dinners [blog], October 23, 2012, http://neverseconds.blogspot.com/2012/10/goodbye-and-thanks-from-harshi.html.

47. Rainey, Good, and Alleyne, "School Dinner Blogger Martha Payne Explains It."

48. Lisa Mullins, "Photo Ban for Nine-Year-Old School Lunch Blogger Lifted," PRI's The World [audio interview], June 15, 2012, http://www.theworld.org/2012/06/neverseconds-blog/, §10.

49. Alice Waters, Chez Panisse, http://www.chezpanisse.com/about/alice-waters/.

50. The Edible Schoolyard Project, "Our History," http://edibleschoolyard.org/our-story.

51. Alice Waters: Edible Education [video], Lisa Eisner, 2011, http://www.nowness.com/day/2011/8/24/1596/alice-waters-edible-education.

52. The Edible Schoolyard Project, http://edibleschoolyard.org/.

53. The Edible Schoolyard, "Eighth Grade Garden Scope and Sequence," 2013, http://edibleschoolyard.org/resource/8th-grade-garden-scope-and-sequence.

54. The Edible Schoolyard, "Eighth Grade Garden Scope and Sequence."

55. Sarah Henry, "New Edible Schoolyard Head Heron Plans for Growth," *Berkeleyside*, October 26, 2012, http://www.berkeleyside.com/2012/10/26/katrina-heron-new-director-of-edible-schoolyard-project/.

56. Waters, "Chez Panisse."

57. USDHHS, *National Action Plan to Improve Health Literacy*, 8.

58. Joan Wharf Higgins and Deborah Begoray, "Exploring the Borderlands between Media and Health: Conceptualizing 'Critical Media Health Literacy,'" *Journal of Media Literacy Education* 4, no. 2 (2012): 136–48, 140.

59. Yale School of Medicine. Comer School Development Program, "About Us," http://medicine.yale.edu/childstudy/comer/about/index.aspx. Accessed November 1, 2014.

60. Lawrence St. Leger, Ian Young, Claire Blanchard, and Martha Perry, *Promoting Health in Schools: From Evidence to Action*. Saint Denis Cedex, France: International Union for Health Promotion and Education, 2010.

61. Susan Wile Schwarz and Yumiko Aratani, *Improving the Odds for Adolescents: State Policies That Support Adolescent Health and Well-Being*. New York: National Center for Children in Poverty, July 2011, 4.

62. Schwarz and Aratani, *Improving the Odds for Adolescents*, 4.

SIX

It Takes a Village

Marilyn Rhames is a writing teacher at a health and wellness charter school on Chicago's South Side. Seven years ago her principal founded the school to provide high quality urban education while also combating the escalating rates of childhood obesity.[1] The school serves 450 students who start the day with the staff with a ten-minute Morning Movement exercise routine. The school has three gyms, one of which is a fully equipped fitness center. Five full-time physical educators provide sixty minutes of physical education to every student Monday through Thursday and forty minutes on Fridays. School lunch is cooked daily and includes a vegetarian option and a salad bar. The school focus on health and wellness is both timely and relevant to the urban Chicago that has an obesity rate higher than the national average.

Not only is Rhames a seasoned educator of nine years, she is a former journalist for *People* and *Time* and a recipient of various awards during her work as a reporter for *Newsday* and *The Journal News* in New York. She is also an award-winning blogger for *Education Week Teacher*. In 2011 she earnestly wrote in a blog post titled, "I Am Overweight: An Authentic Assessment" about her own health struggles:

> Having an overweight teacher at such a health-conscience school is not ironic. It's realistic. I doubt my students ever feel the way my mother did when her 400-pound doctor chastised her for gaining a few pounds between visits. My students can relate to my private temptations with chocolate cake and potato chips because most of them struggle with it, too. Practicing moderation is a skill that takes lots of discipline in our self-indulgent, junk food laden society. So we have to educate ourselves and constantly encourage each other to eat right and stay fit. For example, I push myself to take the stairs to avoid having my students remind me that it burns more calories than riding the elevator.[2]

Rhames's experience is not unlike those of other educators and students who struggle themselves with enacting healthy behaviors. For millions of teachers like Rhames, it is an uphill climb. Participating in regular physical activity at a level sufficient to promote health-related physical fitness is an important behavior for professionals in all fields, including K–12 teachers. At the same time, classroom teachers are expected to master their subject area(s) and to be experts in the art and science of pedagogy. If we are now requiring teachers to model and facilitate health literacy skills and behaviors then they, like their students, cannot do it alone.

MAPPING THE VILLAGE

What are the roles and responsibilities of other educational partners that exist within the ecosystem of teenagers? Since the 1990s this question and others have been central to the work of Dr. Joyce L. Epstein, founder of the National Network of Partnership Schools at Johns Hopkins University. Epstein's work centers on helping schools, districts, and states develop comprehensive school, family, and community partnership programs as part of their school improvement efforts.[3] The idea is that school, family, and community partnerships are an essential component of district leadership and school and classroom organization.

This chapter describes just a few of the stakeholders and programs that currently exist to support healthy teens and healthy schools. These include families, peers, community organizations, school-university partnerships, and industry professionals. Certainly many more partners exist, particularly in the health and medical professions. However, the purpose of this list is to present a typology rather than a comprehensive list. This chapter highlights those partners and programs (both large and small) that actively engage teenagers in their pursuit of health and media literacies. Each of them contributes in a unique and meaningful way to growing healthy teens and healthy schools.

Family Engagement

Research reports that family engagement is the single most accurate predictor of a student's success or failure in school.[4] Family involvement with school has more influence on academic achievement than a child's culture, socioeconomic status, and even family structure.[5] It follows that educators should increase communication between schools and home, provide support for healthy behaviors at home, provide parents with volunteer opportunities at school, and include parents in school decision making.[6]

In 2006 the Healthy Schools Campaign formed Parents United to train parents in organizing school wellness teams and advocacy for healthy changes to school food and fitness. The goal is to connect, engage, and sustain parental involvement. According to their website:

> Over the last eight years, Healthy Schools Campaign has provided training to more than 200 parents and provided tools and support to an additional 1,000 parents in Chicago. These parents have created wellness teams in 55 schools, 25 of which have received recognition from the USDA's HealthierUS School Challenge. In addition, these parents have successfully advocated for district policies related to school food, recess, physical education, nutrition education and district accountability and transparency.[7]

Increased communication with parents about the school environment itself can support behavioral change in their children. A Cornell University initiative involved schools sending home nutritional report cards to parents that resulted in students purchasing fewer cookies and slightly more vegetables and increased their chances of drinking plain instead of flavored milk.[8] The key is proactive scaffolding, including helping parents to discern unhealthy behaviors in their children and make adjustments where needed. Still, parents may not know how to cultivate healthy eating or face serious obstacles in doing so.

Often parents of overweight or obese children do not recognize their child's weight problem. In response, researchers at the North Carolina Children's Hospital provide pediatricians with a "Starting the Conversation" toolkit (consisting of a color-coded body mass index [BMI] chart and series of questions) to help parents. The study showed the most significant improvement in dietary changes among children who were overweight. At follow-up, they were more likely than healthy-weight children to drink lower-fat milk and showed the largest reduction in the frequency of eating out. But overall, children improved fruit and vegetable consumption, decreased sweetened beverages and unhealthy snacks, drank lower-fat milk more, and reduced screen time.[9]

Setting limits on children's media use may not be the best route for parents, however. Research indicates that parental limits and website restriction do not relate to any beneficial outcome to children's Internet use.[10] Rather, the more parents use the Internet with their children, the more frequently their children use the Internet for educational purposes. Young people also learn more from TV when a parent is viewing alongside them and is there to explain what is going on.[11] It is important, then, for educators to provide opportunities (e.g., homework, or Family Night) for families to engage in media and health literacy activities at home with teenagers.

Peer Mentoring

As the formal curriculum in health and physical education within the walls of the school diminishes, an increasingly important mechanism for health literacy among teenagers is peer mentoring. Teenagers who participate in mentoring relationships experience positive academic benefits, including better attendance and better attitudes toward school.[12] Programs that leverage online and offline social networking ensure that adolescent youth evolve into competent communicators and informed leaders, especially in the area of health literacy.[13]

In 1981 after the drunk driving deaths of two teenage hockey players at Wayland High School in Massachusetts, hockey coach Robert Anastas challenged students to be more proactive in doing something about the growing problem of drunk driving. He founded Students Against Driving Drunk (SADD), and along with a group of fifteen students, Anastas developed the Contract for Life, which he would later publish as a book. Teenagers become peer instructors who promote youth safety and health at the local, state, and national levels.

The SADD concept and chapters spread throughout the United States and across the world, and soon thereafter all fifty states passed minimum-age drinking laws and drunk driving fatalities decreased. In 1997, SADD adopted the new name of Students Against Destructive Decisions to encompass the growing number of social pressures facing teens (e.g., alcohol and drug use, suicide, violence, distracted driving). As the organization grew over three decades, it received financial support from corporations, but in 1989 the SADD National Board of Directors voted to cease accepting contributions from the alcohol industry.[14] It is a successful example of peer education and youth leadership—particularly among at-risk youth.

HealthCorps was cofounded by heart surgeon and talk show host Dr. Mehmet Oz and his wife, Lisa Oz. The mission of the organization is "to implement an innovative in-school model that inspires teens to make healthier choices for themselves and their families."[15] HealthCorps peer mentoring service is an in-school health program run by recent college graduates to educate and inspire teenagers to eat healthier, such as reducing consumption of sugary beverages and increasing physical activity. HealthCorps coordinators carry out in-school and community programming in nutrition, fitness, and mental strength that target high-needs populations.

The HealthCorps social network, "TeenDailyStrength," provides teen-focused support groups, a mechanism for sharing experiences with other teens, professional health bloggers, and a mechanism for journaling and posting photos.[16] The web content is in body, mind, and lifestyle from understanding anatomy and building time management skills, to exercise and nutrition. HealthCorps is currently in sixty-six high schools in fourteen states and the District of Columbia.[17]

The Youth Health Literacy Project is a nonprofit project of adults and students in New Mexico that work in partnership to improve the health and reduce health disparities of adolescents by improving their health literacy through social media. The project brings together school-based health centers, youth engagement organizations, and school health advisory councils to help teenagers use and develop health memes through social media applications like Facebook and Twitter to improve their access to accurate medical and health information and dissemination of messages to other youth and families. One of the outcomes is to prepare student health leaders within schools that participate in the project.

Farm to School

The National Farm to School Network (NFSN) was formed in 2007 as an outgrowth of a growing farm to school movement that emerged in the late 1990s and grew to approximately forty thousand schools in all fifty states as of 2012.[18] The NFSN helps communities bring local food sourcing and food and agriculture education in school systems. Network members advocate for policy, volunteer in their local communities, and donate financially. Students gain access to local foods, school gardens, cooking lessons, and farm field trips. State networks provide support through webinars, online communities, and resource connections. Educators need assistance in applying for grants to cover the costs of planting and maintaining a garden. They also need help meeting food safety regulations associated with using garden produce in school meals. Teachers need support in developing lessons that integrate school gardening into their subject area curriculum.

One farm to school resource connection is FoodCorps, a national nonprofit organization that began on Earth Day 2009 when President Obama signed the Kennedy Serve American Act into law. As a partner of AmeriCorps, FoodCorps recruits, trains, and places "emerging leaders" into limited-resource schools for a year of service that implements their "three-ingredient recipe" for healthy kids: 1) give hands-on lessons about food and nutrition; 2) build and tend school gardens and teach cooking lessons; and 3) implement change in school lunches that includes food from local farms.[19]

The momentum of the farm to school movement is making an impact at the state school policy level. In 2003, 2006, and 2011, San Francisco voters passed a bond measure that approved the design and construction of green schoolyards for eighty-three San Francisco Unified School District elementary, middle, and high schools. This is the first urban school district to subscribe to outdoor learning and one of the first large districts in the state to implement the Common Core State Standards.

Wholesome Wave is a national nonprofit that helps underserved communities gain access to local food with incentive programs. Their Fruit and Vegetable Prescription Program (FVRx) helps low-income families encourage healthy eating by providing a "prescription" for subsidized items from the local farmers' market.[20] Doctors enroll overweight and obese children as FVRx participants and together they set healthy goals for eating over a four- to six-month period. Each family receives one dollar per family member per day to spend at local markets. A monthly doctor's visit refills the prescription and resets new healthy eating goals. The program began in 2011 with more than one thousand people in California, Maine, Massachusetts, and Rhode Island, and during the four-month program, more than one-third of the participants experienced a decrease in BMI. Participants also significantly increased their knowledge about their neighborhood farmers' markets, where to buy locally grown produce, and the importance of fruits and vegetables in their diet. [21]

Other grassroots movements like Food Day (fooday.org) appeal to both individual empowerment as well as policy-level changes. The World Health Organization (WHO) designated October 24th as Food Day. The website provides a screening guide and lists of films and companion websites to commemorate the occasion. The idea is to view and then mobilize community engagement around multiple causes. The screening guides contain a list of open access TV segments, commercials, and public service announcements (PSAs) that teachers can use to initiate classroom dialogue.

Culinary Professionals

Since 2007, the Healthy Schools Campaign Cooking Up Change has involved students in the national conversation about school food. The students were challenged with creating a healthy school meal using ingredients common in school kitchens. Teams of high school student chefs from across the United States compete locally, and then the winners convene in Washington, D.C., to advocate for healthier school lunches. Student cooks gave heed to peer feedback, cultural influences, and of course health and nutrition. Some of the student meals have gone on to be a part of the regular school lunch rotation in their home school districts.[22]

A new component of Michelle Obama's *Let's Move!* initiative was *Chefs Move to Schools*, an effort to teach culinary skills to students and to acclimate them on healthy food options. As of 2012, approximately 3,500 schools were partnering with professional chefs to develop healthy school menus and to educate students about a healthier diet. Among the partners of *Chefs Move to Schools* are the United States Department of Agriculture (USDA), Cornell University, Partnership for a Healthier America, and Harvard School of Public Health.

School-University Partnerships

Postsecondary programs in teacher education, educational leadership, public health, nutrition, child advocacy, and health communication are integral in preparing educators for the challenge of health literacy education. The idea is to develop "expert educators" with intersecting educational skills who can serve as role models, mentors, and teachers of health literacy skills to others. Educators can benefit by joining research efforts with colleagues across the disciplines of education, humanities, social sciences, and the medical sciences.[23]

Harvard University Dining Services established the Food Literacy Project in 2004, with a mission to educate students about their food choices, nutrition, sustainability, and food preparation. The Food Literacy Project runs a farmers' market on campus, employs a student in every house to serve as a Food Literacy Project Representative, organizes cooking classes with each house chef and guest chefs, and hosts talks, movie screenings, and tastings.

The Harvard Law School Food Law and Policy Clinic in partnership with the Community Food Security Coalition published a food policy toolkit in July 2012 to provide food policy councils a foundational understanding of basic legal concepts surrounding local food systems, develop a base of knowledge about the main policy areas, and discover examples and innovations from other cities and states. The toolkit supports local organizations to initiate change within their local food systems by connecting schools with local farmers and producers and advocating for nutrition education and farm to school programs.

Nonprofit Alliances

The American Heart Association and the Clinton Foundation in 2006 established the Alliance for a Healthier Generation (AHG) in response to the growing rate of childhood obesity. The Robert Wood Johnson Foundation provided an initial $8 million to start the Healthy Schools Program, recently awarding a $20 million grant to expand the program to over eight thousand schools in states with the highest obesity rates. The specific goal is "to create systemic change, change that is not isolated to one home, or community, to one school, industry, or state."[24] The Healthy School Program is in twenty-six thousand schools in every state and provides a Healthy Out-of-School Time Framework to address healthy eating and physical activity standards. The AHG has also brokered voluntary agreements with the beverage, snack food, dairy, fitness, and healthcare industries. The agreements are for companies to create products and services that meet nutrition guidelines and physical activity standards. AHG states that they will not accept money from businesses with which they are "negotiating solutions."[25]

Media Advocates

Melinda Hemmelgarn, also known as The Food Sleuth, is a registered dietitian, investigative nutritionist, and advocate for social environmental justice. As a freelance writer and weekly syndicated Internet radio host, Hemmelgarn's mission is to "help people think beyond their plates, connect the dots between food, health and agriculture; and, promote critical thinking and food system literacy."[26] Her Food Sleuth Radio program airs live on www.kopn.org every Thursday and features guests such as NSFN leaders, authors, experts on genetically modified organisms (GMOs), and chefs. Hemmelgarn is a pioneer of connecting food literacy and media literacy. Her columns and radio programs inspire young people to be both critical food consumers and creative media artists.

Dr. Kevin Strong, a pediatrician in Camden, Maine, founded Dunk the Junk to educate teens—through graffiti, hip-hop, and acrobatic slam dunks—about the dangers of excessive junk food consumption. He emphasizes eliminating sugar from the diet, especially sugar contained in beverages. Dunk the Junk offers on its website an animated "Top 10 Foods to Dunk Out of Your Diet" featuring graffiti art by Mike Rich and dunking by 2011 College Dunk Champion Jacob Tucker. The website offers other "cool" merchandise with the Dunk the Junk messaging that appeal to teenagers.

Over the past decade, health literacy and media literacy have been the focus of a growing collaboration among schools, families, community organizations, local farmers, local government, higher education, and youth development agencies, among others, to provide educational opportunities for teenagers. From this perspective, fostering health literacy may be more a matter of informal education within a larger system than it is a matter of formal school curriculum.

BEYOND THE VILLAGE

The social, political, and economic determinants of health trump the scientific knowledge and our ability to act on that knowledge. Corporate interests sway research findings, co-opt philanthropy for marketing purposes, persuade voters to oppose public health regulation, and lobby politicians to oppose industry regulation. Local, state, and federal governments bow to special interests, and the economic imperative reigns supreme. These tensions and contradictions pose real challenges to adolescent youth who actively participate in popular culture and to a much lesser extent in politics. It begs the question, "What are the roles and responsibilities of corporations and the federal and state governments (including schools) in promoting adolescent health literacy?"

The importance of holding all economic, political, social, and commercial institutions accountable for public health cannot be understated, given that public health throughout history is inextricably connected to the political and social agendas of the dominant power structure.

There is an unrealistic expectation that health literate behaviors can occur without adjusting the sociopolitical environment. We can learn much from health researchers of childhood obesity. "It's not really so hard to change an overweight child's environment and to see big improvements in habits and overall health."[27] Similarly, if we pay attention to how our educational ecologies shape the health of young people in the United States, improvements are also more likely to occur with simple changes to the ecosystem of teenagers.

As one of the last bastions of democracy, public schools are the places where these conversations and actions can intentionally and should systematically occur. Young people should learn how to civilly dissent, deliberate, debate, and to enact moral and evidence-based decision making about their physical, social, and mental health. If the public purpose of schooling in the United States is to cultivate healthy and responsible citizens, then it follows that educators *at all levels* must imbue media and health literacies. Furthermore, if life, liberty, and the pursuit of happiness are to be tangible realities rather than abstract principles, then the ability for educators to engage in interdisciplinary research and praxis is crucial.

Given the bureaucratic constraints of reduced funding for schools and a shrinking curriculum, it is essential that schools create and sustain effective partnerships with community organizations and out of school and after-school programs. Grafting in more community agencies and organizations as partners can help prepare community leaders and educators to find ways to bridge the digital and health divides that still exist in impoverished communities across the United States.

Australian health researcher Lawrence St. Leger summarizes the seemingly immense expectations placed on schools. He writes, "We are still unclear about what outcomes we expect [schools] to achieve. Is it behaviour change, new knowledge, technical skills, community action competencies, physical health advances, or all of these plus others?"[28] If it is all of the above, then we need physical, social, and curriculum structures that support these goals. In short, we need a village.

NOTES

1. Marilyn Rhames, "I Am Overweight: An Authentic Assessment." Charting My Own Course (blog), *Education Week*, September 21, 2011, http://blogs.edweek.org/teachers/charting_my_own_course/2011/09/i_am_overweight.html. Accessed August 3, 2013.

2. Rhames, "I Am Overweight."

3. Holly Kreider, "The National Network of Partnership Schools: A Model for Family-School-Community Partnerships," May 2000, Harvard Family Research Project.

4. Jacquelynne S. Eccles and Rena D. Harold, "Family Involvement in Children's and Adolescents' Schooling," in *Family School Links*, eds. Alan Booth and Judith F. Dunn, 3–34. Mahwah, NJ: Lawrence Erlbaum Associates, 1996.

5. Anne T. Henderson and Karen L. Mapp, *A New Wave of Evidence: The Impact of School, Family, and Community Connections on Student Achievement*. Austin, TX: National Center for Family and Community Connections with Schools, 2002; William H. Jeynes, "A Meta-Analysis: The Effects of Parental Involvement on Minority Children's Academic Achievement," *Education and Urban Society* 35, no. 2 (2003): 202–18.

6. Janet L. Epstein, L. Coates, K. C. Salinas, M. G. Sanders, and B. S. Simon, *School, Family, and Community Partnerships: Your Handbook for Action*. Thousand Oaks, CA: Corwin Press, 1997.

7. Healthy Schools Campaign, "Parent Empowerment: An Effective Strategy for Improving School Food and Fitness," http://www.healthyschampaign.org/programs/parents-united/. Accessed November 6, 2014.

8. http://www.smarterlunchrooms.org.

9. Eliana M. Perrin, Julie C. Jacobson Vann, John T. Benjamin, Asheley Cockrell Skinner, Steven Wagner, and Alice S. Ammerman, "Use of a Pediatrician Toolkit to Address Parental Perception of Children's Weight Status, Nutrition, and Activity Behaviors," *Academic Pediatrics* 10 (2010): 274–81.

10. S. Lee and Y. Chae, "Children's Internet Use in a Family Context: Influence on Family Relationships and Parental Mediation," *CyberPsychology & Behavior* 10 (2007): 640–44.

11. Lori Takeuchi, "Families Matter: Designing Media for a Digital Age," Joan Ganz Cooney Center at Sesame Workshop, June 2011, http://www.joanganzcooneycenter.org/publication/families-matter-designing-media-for-a-digital-age/. Accessed January 18, 2013.

12. Jennifer M. Good, Glennelle Halpin, and Gerald Halpin, "A Promising Prospect for Minority Retention: Students Becoming Peer Mentors," *Journal of Negro Education* 69 (2000): 375–83.

13. Angela Cooke Jackson and Kaitlin Barnes, "Peer-to-Peer Mentoring among Urban Youth: The Intersection of Health Communication, Media Literacy and Digital Health Vignettes," *Journal of Digital and Media Literacy*, December 2013, http://www.jodml.org/2013/12/01/peer-to-peer-mentoring-among-urban-youth-the-intersection-of-health-communication-media-literacy-and-digital-health-vignettes/.

14. "History of SADD," SADD Profile, http://sadd.org/history.htm.

15. Healthcorps, "About," http://healthcorps.org/who-we-are/about/. Accessed January 18, 2013.

16. See http://www.dailystrength.org/features/teenDailyStrength.

17. Healthcorps, "About," §3.

18. About The National Farm to School Network http://www.farmtoschool.org/about. Accessed November 5, 2014.

19. FoodCorps, "About Us," https://foodcorps.org/about. Accessed November 5, 2014.

20. Wholesome Wave, Fruit and Vegetable Prescription Program (FVRx), http://www.wholesomewave.org/our-initiatives/fruit-and-vegetable-prescription-program/. Accessed November 4, 2014.

21. Wholesome Wave.

22. Rochelle Davis, "High School Students Cooking Up Change," Jamie Oliver's Food Revolution [blog], http://www.jamieoliver.com/us/foundation/jamies-food-revolution/news-content/high-school-chefs-are-rewriting-the-reci. Accessed August 8, 2013.

23. Marcus B. Weaver-Hightower, "Why Education Researchers Should Take School Food Seriously," *Educational Researcher* 40 (2011): 15–21, doi: 10.3102/

0013189X10397043. Lynda Bergsma, "Media Literacy and Health Promotion for Adolescents," *Journal of Media Literacy Education* 3, no. 1 (2011): 25–28.

24. Alliance for a Healthier Generation, "Our Story," https://www.healthiergeneration.org/about_us/our_story/. Accessed November 2, 2014.

25. Alliance for a Healthier Generation, "About Us," https://www.healthiergeneration.org/about_us/.

26. Melinda Hemmelgarn, Blogger Profile, https://www.blogger.com/profile/02226561139153125293.

27. Susan Okie, *Fed Up! Winning the War against Childhood Obesity*. Washington, DC: Joseph Henry Press, 2005.

28. Lawrence St. Leger, "What's the Place of Schools in Promoting Health? Are We Too Optimistic?" *Health Promotion International* 19, no. 4 (2004): 408, doi: 10.1093/heapro/dah401.

Index

academic achievement, 9; link to obesity, 21; relation to health, 88–89, 98

addiction: information about, 61; to nicotine, 1; to sugar, 1–2

adolescence: adult perspectives of, 8, 25; agency, 8; challenges of, 7, 9; cognitive development, 57, 68; consumer culture, 36; definition of, 7; ecology of, 93, 104, 111; lack of health literacy, 8; length of, 8; media portrayal of, 39; opportunities as adults, 25; optimism towards future, 25; parental relationships, 19; physical changes of, 7; risks of, 3; social changes within, 7–8, 35; violence in, 19

advertising: alcohol, 45, 82; during the late 1700s, 35; emergence of, 33–34; for fast food, 18; for sugary drinks, 18, 74; in high schools, 36–37, 43, 80, 82; nutritional, 64–65; online, 56; targeting teens, 18, 43, 82. *See also* Television, as a medium for classroom instruction; Whittle Communications

Affordable Care Act, 76; in community change, 7; of consumer, 77; in learning, 10, 11; in media consumption, 6, 45–46, 63; over physical body, 19, 98; and social change, 6, 63; threats to, 19

alcohol: advertising of, 45; concerns about abuse, 18; prevention of use, 11, 42, 47, 106; risks compared to obesity, 21; teen uses of, 35

alcohol and drug prevention, 9, 42

Alcott, William, 34

AllerSchool System, 57

Alliance for a Healthier Generation, 109

Alliance to Feed the Future, 66

AmeriCorps. *See* FoodCorps.

American Academy of Family Physicians, 75

American Academy of Pediatrics, 3, 47, 76

American Association of Health Education, 100n5

American Beverage Association, 76

American Civil War, 35

American Dream, 4

American Heart Association, 109

American Legacy Foundation, 47

Americanization of immigrants, 36

American Medical Association, 4; definition of health literacy, 4; classification of obesity, 20

American Physiological Society, 34

apprenticeships, 97

Association for Supervision and Curriculum Development, 99

astroturfing, 66

audience, 37, 38, 40, 43, 46, 47, 48, 49, 55, 63–64, 65, 67, 68. *See also* media messages

Austin, Erica, 57

automobile: importance of, 35; transportation, 18

Begoray, Deborah, 10

Beyoncé. *See* Carter, Beyoncé Knowles

blogging, 6, 55, 93–94, 103, 106

Bloomberg, Michael, 77

body mass index (BMI), 20; definition of, 20; questions of validity, 20; measurement of, 59, 105

broadcast media, 37–43, 55

Budweiser, 74, 82

bullying, 18, 61, 88

caffeine: excessive intake, 1–4, 16; toxicity, 3
canteens, 39
capitalism, 19
cardiac arrest, 3
cardiac arrhythmia, 1–3
cardiovascular health, 20
Carter, Beyoncé Knowles, 74, 82–83
celebrity endorsement, 74, 82–83, 87, 94
censorship, 37; federal policies, 45; of motion pictures, 37–39; of music, 39–40; of TV content, 41. *See also* protectionism
Center for Consumer Freedom, 66
Center for Ecoliteracy, 96
Center for Science in the Public Interest, 17, 57, 75, 76
Centers for Disease Control and Prevention, 16, 19, 24, 28n35, 47
Channel One, 43
Chefs Move to Schools, 108
child labor laws, 36
childhood obesity. *See* obesity
Children's Online Privacy Protection Act (COPPA), 56
Children's Television Act, 47
cholera, 34
citizen journalists, 23
citizenship, 6
Clinton Foundation, 109. *See also* Alliance for a Healthier Generation.
Coca-Cola, 1; advertising in schools, 43, 79, 80, 82; anti-obesity campaign, 67, 75; canteens, 39; corporate interests, 6, 76; cultural symbolism of, 2; dependence on workers' health, 24; excessive drinking of, 1–2; facebook fans, 2–3; invention of, 35; marketing of, 78, 84n8; news headlines, 2; rewards program, 56; share of Monster, 12n21
coffee consumption, 16, 67
Cohen, Carolyn, 92
Coke. *See* Coca-Cola
Collins, Mary, 18
Comer, James, 98

Common Core Curriculum Standards, 96, 107
Community Food Security Coalition, 109
community programs, 11
consumer behavior, 81
cookies, 56
cooking skills, 6, 17, 65, 92, 95, 107, 108, 109
Coordinated School Health Program, 98. *See also* whole school model.
corporate lobbying, 75, 110
corporate practices, 4, 82, 109; impeding agency, 4
counter-cultural resistance, 11
critical media health literacy, 57, 68
critical thinking. *See* media literacy
cultural studies, 68
curriculum standards, 88
cyber safety, 88

data personalization, 59–60
death: accidental poisoning, 16; among smokers, 20; drunk driving fatalities, 46; homicide, 19; motor vehicle collisions, 16; painkillers, 16
democracy in schooling, 10, 111
Democratic Voter's Choice, 66
diabetes, 20
diet books, 24
diets: apps for, 57, 59; dangers of, 24; relation to TV viewing, 45
digital media: literacy, 6; prevents physical exercise, 19; uses among children, 19; uses among teens, 55
documentary films, 23
driver's education, 9
Dunk the Junk, 110

eating disorders, 45, 92. *See also* diets
eating out, 17
edible education, 97
Edible Schoolyard, 95–97
Ellington, Duke, 74
emotional illiteracy, 16. *See also* health, emotional
Epstein, Joyce L., 104
European Union, 20
Evans, John, 92

starvation, 17
St. Leger, Lawrence, 10, 111
stereotyping, 65
stress management, 61
Strong, Kevin, 110
student growth objectives, 88
Students Against Driving Drunk
    (SADD), 46, 106
sugar, 1; in cheap foods, 23; excessive
    intake, 1, 15–16; public health threat
    of, 19; reducing consumption, 15,
    75, 91
suicide, 92
supermarkets, 17, 66
Supplemental Nutrition Assistance
    Program, 76
Surgeon General, 15, 42–43, 81
Swiss Beatz, 74

technological development, 11, 17, 18,
    26, 33, 35, 37–49, 44, 46, 49, 58, 59,
    60, 68, 88
teen pregnancy, 18
Telecommunications Act, 45
television: as a commercial medium,
    40–41, 43, 47; as the common school,
    43; emergence of, 37, 40; impact of,
    41–42, 44, 44–45; as least elite
    medium, 63; as a medium of
    classroom instruction, 41–43, 43;
    promotion of, 42; sexual content, 45;
    viewing among teens, 18, 63
temperance, 34
texting, 55, 59
time management, 106
tobacco: adult concerns, 18; advertising
    of, 41, 65; campaigns against use, 11,
    47, 48; politics of, 66; risks
    compared to obesity, 21
transmedia, 6, 61, 62
Twitter, 56, 58, 60, 79, 94, 107

UK National Child Development
    Study, 89
United Nations, 78

United Nations Non-Communicable
    Diseases Action Group, 67, 76, 78
United States: as an obesigenic culture,
    20; internal struggle, 19;
    institutional forces, 19
U.S. Department of Agriculture, 78–79,
    79, 80, 108
U.S. Department of Health and Human
    Services, 20, 47, 90, 98
U.S. Farmers and Ranchers Alliance, 66

vaccinations, 48
veganism.. *See also* vegetarianism, 34
Vegetable Prescription Program, 108
video games, 46; in promoting health,
    46; use of, 63; in neighborhoods, 18;
    on TV, 42, 45

Walmart, 24
Wansink, Brian, 81
Warner, Melanie, 17, 64
warning labels, 1, 3; moving beyond, 9;
    understanding of, 4, 62, 64
Wartella, Ellen, 44
Waters, Alice, 95–97
Weaver-Hightower, 80
weight gain: relationship to TV
    viewing on, 44
weight loss : apps for, 59, 61; industry,
    24; research on, 22
Weis, DaraLynn, 21
Wharf Higgins, Joan, 10
White House Conference on Children
    and Youth, 42
Whittle Communications, 43
whole school model, 98–99
Wholesome Wave, 108
Weight Watchers, 24
World Health Organization, 4, 20, 25,
    73, 76
world population, 20

Yale Rudd Center for Food Policy, 18
Youth Health Literacy Project, 107
Youth leadership, 46

49457331R00080

Made in the USA
Lexington, KY
06 February 2016